"Why Me? Why Not Me"

Captain Bob's journey to heaven through surrender.

ROBERT R. SCHULTE

WestBow
PRESS
A DIVISION OF THOMAS NELSON

ISBN: 978-1-4497-6822-5 (sc)
ISBN: 978-1-4497-6823-2 (hc)
ISBN: 978-1-4497-6821-8 (e)

Library of Congress Control Number: 2012917712

WestBow Press books may be ordered through booksellers or by contacting:

WestBow Press
A Division of Thomas Nelson
1663 Liberty Drive
Bloomington, IN 47403
www.westbowpress.com
1-(866) 928-1240

Printed in the United States of America

WestBow Press rev. date: 11/29/2012

Forward
by
Cindy Schulte

Why me, God? Why not me? I noticed a swelling on my lower left leg on the calf muscle in late December 2009. There was no pain at all, so I dismissed it as a swelling from a hard fall I had taken in my basement about a month earlier. I showed it to Cindy, who wanted me to go to the doctor; however, if you haven't noticed, I am thickheaded, and I wanted to see if it would just go away. It didn't.

The doctor's visit and subsequent MRI in February began the process of identifying just what this thing was. Treatment could only begin after a positive ID. At this point, I was not overly concerned. I still believed it to be a hematoma from the fall. It turned out to be much, much more.

This is the first entry into a 2-year CaringBridge.org journal for my husband Bob who was 63 at the time and a very virile and active man. The hematoma turned out to be a rare and aggressive cancer that would take his life just 2 years later. The journal documents the tremendous faith and strength that he received from Christ every step of the way. The journal will carry you through the innermost thoughts of a man who knows that there is a possibility that he will not live through this, but turns to God and sees the joy of life in adversity. I rode the journey with him for 2 years and realized that through Jesus, Bob was able to not only live well but also to die well. His journal will put you front and center on his beautiful journey, something he called "an e-ticket ride with Christ." This online blog allowed his friends and family to encourage him by contributing comments through the guestbook. We were all blessed to be a part of his journey and I hope, that after reading this, you will feel blessed too.

Chapter 1

THE JOURNEY BEGINS

WRITTEN FEBRUARY 2, 2010, 9:40 A.M.

The doctor sent me for an MRI at the Hospital of Central Connecticut in New Britain. Scanning my left leg to try to identify what this thing is. Still no pain at all. We hope it is a hematoma caused by my fall and the fact that I am on blood thinners.

WRITTEN FEBRUARY 5, 2010, 9:43 A.M.

MRI results are suspicious. Not a hematoma. The doctor now wants to turn it over to a surgeon for biopsy and follow-up. Don't much like that B word.

Our vacation to Quebec City and the Winter Carnival is next week. The trip is a gift from me to Cindy for her sixtieth birthday. I want to go, so the biopsy is scheduled for the following week on 2/16/2010.

WRITTEN FEBRUARY 16, 2010, 9:48 A.M.

Quebec City was great fun. We loved our stay at the Chateau Frontenac, but today is the biopsy. The procedure is a snap, and they give you a little medicine so it's only a blur in your memory. No pain. The nurses said results would be in three to five working days. Each day felt like it was a hundred hours long, and answering phone calls was tough when I had no info.

WRITTEN FEBRUARY 23, 2010, 9:52 A.M.

February 23rd. They past few days have been difficult not knowing, but we are beginning to think the worst.

Update: The doctor's office just called, and they said they have the results and that the doctor wanted to discuss them with us in his office in two days. That was when we knew we had problems.

WRITTEN FEBRUARY 25, 2010, 9:56 A.M.

I like Dr. FL a lot, but he had nothing good to say. He scheduled me for emergency surgery on *next Tuesday*, March 2nd. First, a whole battery of tests: pre-op blood tests, pre-op physical, EKG, and echocardiogram. Stop the blood thinners and test their level now. Notify my cardiologist, etc. Tomorrow, pre-op screening at the hospital and a CAT scan of the chest and lungs.

WRITTEN FEBRUARY 26, 2010, 10:02 A.M.

Visited Hospital of Central Connecticut for the pre-op and CAT scan testing. Saw nurse Laura there, and she promised to stop in next week after the surgery. Things moving along fast now. The operation is labeled, "left-leg reconstruction!" I don't like that name at all!

It is a big tumor, about 13 centimeters. The doctor has to take a big part of my lower leg, including the calf muscle, peroneal nerve, and perhaps even the fibula bone. The doctor said I don't need that bone and it is often harvested to reconstruct people's jaws and other bony structures. I will have to use some sort of appliance to assist me for something called "drop foot." Concerned about the surgery but placing our trust in God, we began praying Romans 8:28.

WRITTEN FEBRUARY 28, 2010, 10:20 A.M.

Church was written for me today. I especially loved the hymn that Marcel and Amy did. It was a great job, and I hope we see a hymn featured often!

People who know what is going on are praying and want to stay in the loop. I am getting a lot of support now ... thank you.

I am strangely calm about this whole thing. I just want this to work for the glory of God. I don't know if I have ever actually influenced someone to make a decision for Jesus, but it has always been my desire to be an instrument of God in that regard. I really know that I am saved, so I tell people that it is a win-win situation for me.

My doctor doesn't talk about "five-year survival"; however, I did research on the web, and the numbers seem to be in the neighborhood of fifty-fifty. Not really happy with that. The doctor is concerned about hemotropic spreading of the disease through the bloodstream. That's why he is working fast and plans an aggressive operation.

WRITTEN MARCH 1, 2010, 10:35 A.M.

Just got hit with a sledge hammer. More later.

WRITTEN MARCH 1, 2010, 10:22 P.M.

The CAT scan showed three hot spots on my right lung that are consistent with the way this type of cancer spreads. The doctor canceled my Tuesday operation so the lungs could be addressed first. They have my undivided attention now, Lord. Are You watching?

WRITTEN MARCH 2, 2010, 10:25 A.M.

This is *crazy*. Last night was the worst. We really thought I had bought the farm. Midmorning, we got a call from the doctor, and they have found an old PET scan from 2008 that also showed the three areas on my lungs. That means that my current cancer did not cause them, and they probably are not cancerous.

This is a roller-coaster ride now!

More doctors this week, and an end-of-week PET scan to put the lung issue to bed once and for all before any treatment plan is implemented. Discussion about perhaps taking the leg at the knee. Probably a better idea than leaving some disfigured appendage that won't work anyway. I have two gold teeth that my grandkids know were made from pirate gold taken in my youth and buried in an old oak tree in the woods behind our house. Maybe a peg leg? I'll become a legend in my own time.

People's best wishes are pouring in with promises of prayer. I really feel held up. We continue to pray Romans 8:28.

WRITTEN MARCH 3, 2010, 9:55 P.M.

Today we met with our oncologist. She is a female doctor and very professional. She immediately put us at rest with her methods. Because the tumor is so large, she believes that we should use a mix of surgery, radiation, and chemotherapy. She has promised to get back to us on Friday afternoon after the PET scan is complete and she has had time to argue the case with the surgeon and radiologist.

We hope we find out on Friday, or it will be another long weekend of waiting. Cindy and I are really sure that we made a good decision in taking this problem to New Britain. My personal doctor has practiced there as my doctor since 1972, when I worked for Stanley Tools. He was the one who found my last cancer in my back in 2007.

WRITTEN MARCH 4, 2010, 4:26 P.M.

Today I had a long visit with Dr. G, my oncological radiologist. He mentioned that Dr. FL, my surgeon, and Dr. FA, my oncologist, have been on the phone at least three times this week discussing treatment options. Even though the Internet has a good bit of info on my type of cancer, I found that it still is fairly rare.

We spoke a lot about the probable treatment, but I will not list that here until after the final PET scan tomorrow. What I can tell you is that Dr. G is the most optimistic doctor about my cancer and thinks it can be licked without amputation of the leg.

WRITTEN MARCH 5, 2010, 7:26 P.M.

Big day today—PET scan. The day started with snow. It seems that every day this week when we drove to the hospital or to a doctor's office, we had snow. Today is no different, but at least it is light and hasn't stuck. We have picked out a back route to New Britain with "Margaret's" help. Margaret is my GPS. If you knew my late sister-in-law, you would know why I named the GPS Margaret. Margaret is opinionated and generally very accurate.

The full-body PET-CT scan started out at 9:00 a.m. with an IV. The scan consists of an injection with a radioactive sugar solution and a scan with a device sensitive to radiation—sugar because cancer cells love sugar and radioactive because the PET-CT machine can detect pockets of the radiated sugar in the fast-growing cancer cells. I don't like PET-CT and MRI machines. They are just too constricting. I am a big guy and occasionally suffer from claustrophobia. Today was not good, and at one point, I almost called out to have them "get me outta there." But we made it through, finishing the almost-two-hour test at 12:15. Then the waiting for the results started.

After a short lunch, we went for my one o'clock appointment at the radiologist's. Today, we did a "simulation." They fabricated a "jig," which holds my legs immobile. While my legs are in the jig, the X-ray machine can accurately aim and fire its radiation. They tattooed my leg with four dots that line up with the laser beams they use for aiming the X-ray machine. I was told I would get radiation treatment every day for five weeks, then five weeks off, and then into the hospital for the actual operation to remove the dead tumor, then rehab to learn how to cope with the reduced mobility, which is expected.

We finished with the radiologist at around 3:00 and got home in time to get a call from the doctor. *My lungs are completely clean of cancer!* The three lesions turned out to be old scar tissue. This was the news that so many of my friends have been praying for. Now I can concentrate on just the leg!

WRITTEN MARCH 8, 2010, 8:08. P.M.

The past couple of weeks have been busy, almost a blur of activity. We have not yet gotten comfortable with the fast-paced decision-making and harnessing the emotions that go along with the word "cancer," and we probably never will. I have spent time on the web, speaking to people and researching my cancer. The learning curve has been vertical. There is just so much to learn.

The insurance company has asked me if I would like a registered nurse to help me manage the case. I am as suspicious of the health-care insurance industry as anyone, but right now, an informed assistant is pretty attractive. You are assigned one person to call for everything, including questions with bills, etc. They call doctors with questions as necessary and provide translation services for the medical jargon. I have had one fifteen-minute conversation with her so far and must make a decision to continue or not. It's another thing to pray about before deciding.

This week will be a slow one. No appointments with diabolical machines and no injections with radioactive solutions or dyes. This is a week for getting used to the idea of having cancer and for tying up some loose ends. Until now we were running hard and fast. Now things are slowing down enough to sink in. Next Monday will be my first day of radiation therapy, but we have one more appointment with the radiologist before then. The radiation being delivered to the cancer is manipulated by duration, strength, angle, and shutters so that it is focused on the bad cells and not the good. For example, if radiation with a strength of X is directed onto the cancer from two different angles, 2X can be applied to the cancer and only 1X on the surrounding good tissue. The total treatment plan of twenty-five fractions (treatments) is planned by a physicist and then run by the technicians on a device that measures the total number of "gray" delivered to the cancer. This is all part of the quality controls being used by the Hospital of Central Connecticut. Radiation used to be measured in "rad" and now is measured in "gray." One rad is equal to ten milligray, A hundred rad is equal to one gray.

On Friday of this week, I have to go for photography. If there is anyone out there who knows why they have to photograph my leg, I would like to hear from you.

WRITTEN MARCH 9, 2010, 4:59 P.M.

Richard Fritz, an elementary and high school buddy whom I have not seen since June of 1964, filled me in on the photography. Basically, there will be the typical "before and after" pictures, which may help in the treatment but cannot help if I don't take them. At the same time, they check to see how the leg "jig" fits on the actual machine we will be using. Thanks, Rich, and I look forward to seeing you at the Sacred Heart School all-classes reunion on April 24th.

Today I had a nice conversation with my surgeon, Dr. FL. He has been doing some consulting with a nationally renowned colleague down in Philadelphia, and it is that consultation that resulted in the "radiation first" approach instead of the other way around. He has also never dealt with a representative of the insurance company before, didn't say not to, but put me on to a personal nurse navigator who works in the cancer center and works with cancer patients. I think I like my own contacts better than the insurance company's. One turnoff in the literature the insurance company sent to me, was several mentions about their being able to recommend "alternative" treatment and assist me in containing the expenses.

The way I feel about this deal is that once you assemble your team—and I have a great one—and pick a hospital, my favorite one locally, run with the treatment and to Hades with the expenses!

Written March 11, 2010, 7:50 a.m.

I find it interesting that I have to compartmentalize my thought processes in order to be productive. When I allow everything I have to do to be on the table at one time, I can't seem to get my arms around it all. If I calm down and think about one thing at a time, I do okay. I never was very good at multitasking, but I am doing worse now. I have to force myself to live up to some of the commitments I have made to others. I am afraid that I might not force myself once the fatigue that the doctors are saying is coming is upon me.

When I was in the hospital for one of my scans, the nurse administering the meds to keep me calm told me she had to double-dose me because though I may have been calm on the surface, I couldn't hide the tension underneath from my heart and nerves. Her comment struck home. I have had high blood pressure for years and have always considered it a weakness. I wish I could feel internally as calm as I feel on the surface.

By the way, I want to thank you all for the nearly three hundred visits to this website and the hundred or so people that have made them. I especially want to thank the people who wrote messages of encouragement. You have no idea how much enjoyment a narcissist derives from such readings.

WRITTEN MARCH 11, 2010, 8:03 P.M.

March 11th was a great day in the website "guestbook." I hope those of you who have not peeked will take a look and read the "guestbook." There is some real wisdom coming through in people's comments. Thank you so much.

CariAnne, I do need to clarify one thing. The lady sounding so much like my mom is really Cindy's mom and my mother-in-law. I have called her mom as a title of respect for many years. Her name is Helen. My mom, also named Helen, died ten years ago at the age of eighty-nine. She was a matriarch in our family and is much missed. Our family has been blessed with strong women who kept the brothers and sons and nephews and uncles speaking to one another and who have a knack for walking carefully through the minefield of "in-law" relationships.

I hoped that the website would reduce the communication burden, but I never thought that it could become a place to receive such personal wisdom from my friends. I thank you all for that.

Tomorrow is an exciting day for us. I actually have some computer work that must be done for one of my larger accounts. Later in the day is my photo shoot at the radiologist's. (Autographed photos may be available at a later date.) Finally, my daughter, the mother of my grandchildren, Nicolas and Lara, who live in Minneapolis, is flying in alone for a visit. She has promised to bring the kids out after my operation ... so maybe late June or July. I promised in return to start using her name again after I see my grandchildren.

It is going to be a long summer. I am glad we have the big screen HDTV and the house is air-conditioned. There will be a lot of Red Sox games for me to watch! By the way, I loved that Nomar came back for one day so that he could retire a Red Sox. That was honest of him and a classy move by the Sox.

WRITTEN MARCH 12, 2010, 8:06 P.M.

This morning got started (after coffee) with some pretty amazing computer gymnastics. I was in over my head, but with coaching from an IT guru in NYC, we managed to get a client set up on some pretty fancy and secure remote domains. Only about 1 percent of my business is done at this level, so I am terrible at it ... but a good bluff is worth years of school. Or so it seems sometimes.

This afternoon at the cancer center came my photo shoot ... or at least what I thought was going to be a photo shoot. Really, they did call it that. In actuality it was my first meeting with the hardware that they will be using on me. It was a Varian, a computer-controlled, digitized X-ray machine running Trilogy programming command sets. It was a pretty cool-looking machine with the following features.

>> A broad range of external beam therapies, including 3D CRT, IMRT, IGRT, or DART, using the Trilogy system.

>> Multiple dose-rate options—up to 1000mu/min for efficient SRS delivery.

» 2D and 3D KV image guidance for higher-quality imaging at lower doses.

» Full 360-degree range of treatment-delivery angles with positional couch angles.

» Stereotactic frame or frameless immobilization for patient positioning to treat any area of the body.

» Real-time Position Management (RPM) system for gating perfectly timed beam delivery with minimal margins.

» Portal Dosimetry IMRT treatment delivery verification.

» Dynamic high-resolution MLC for exquisite beam sculpting.

» Delivery verification and quality assurance in Argus Linac and Argus IMRT quality-assurance software.

To put it in lay terms, it reminded me of a Mustang that had two Rochester 750 CFM four-barrel carbs set up on an Edelbrock manifold, stuffing as much gas as possible into an eight-cylinder Cleveland 351 CI block. At eleven-to-one compression, it puts out over 400 HP at 3500 RPM. Honest, that is what it looked and sounded like. Well, maybe a little bit anyway.

There I am, strapped in with a five-point seat-belt system so I can't move, and everyone runs for cover, out of the room right after telling me how harmless the radiation is in the dosages I am getting today! So much for honesty.

Finished the day with another blood test, then home in time to welcome my daughter in from Minneapolis and then out to a nice Italian dinner at Iliano's. We saw Chelsea and Brenda there. They both look great!

WRITTEN MARCH 13, 2010, 7:31 P.M.

It's Saturday after lunch. My belly is full. A nap would be great, but the house is full of family. Erica is in from Minneapolis, and my nephew Kurt is up from New Jersey, where most of my relatives live. Kurt is Erica's godfather, so he had a double reason to visit. They both will be going to church tomorrow with us. I appreciate my home on days like this. Rain, wind, and a damp penetrating chill—not cold but penetrating—makes for a real appreciation of good roofing.

The DVD *Polar Express* is playing in the living room in a failed attempt to interest the kids in something other than playing with the adults and singing. Like her mom, Sadie has a great voice but tends to make up more lyrics and hit higher notes.

I have a large pine tree in the backyard that was blown partially down in the windstorm a few weeks ago. It has a large shallow root mass that was pulled up out of the ground, and the tree itself is hung up in other trees at about a 70 degree angle. I have been looking at it for a couple of weeks now, and it hasn't moved an inch. There is no way to get any heavy equipment down there until the ground firms up over my leaching field. The tree is going to have to wait for me to get back on my feet so I can manage the removal. Meanwhile, I think I will ask permission from Rich and Vicki to allow Bennett to walk up the tree from the bottom. Should be fun!

WRITTEN MARCH 14, 2010, 2:10 P.M.

It was good to see so many of you at church this morning and also to have the opportunity to say a few words together. What a nice, busy place today! My daughter, Erica, and my nephew Kurt were there with Cindy and me. Kurt even makes me look short next to him.

Thank you, all, for your prayers and well-wishes. I am excited that tomorrow, I finally get some payback! Up until now, that cancer has been growing and making my leg more and more uncomfortable. Tomorrow, we are going to start shooting it with megawatts of electrical energy converted into radioactive particle beams striking havoc in the cozy confines of the tumor. If you hear screaming at 3:00 p.m. tomorrow, that will be my cancer begging for mercy, and none will be shown. I'm back!

Five weeks of radiation, every weekday, then five weeks off to heal, then the operation. Please save some of your prayers and well-wishes for me when I actually go into the hospital for the surgery. Cindy will need your support then as well. I admit that is the one event I dread.

Chapter 2

THE RADIATION ROLLER-COASTER

WRITTEN MARCH 15, 2010 7:28 P.M.

Today was my most difficult day so far. I'm not in the dumps or even close. But the daily drill that I am embarking on started today, and it seems so long at five weeks ... then five weeks for healing and only then leg reconstruction surgery.

The first full-blown radiation treatment today was a little unnerving. I thought it was going to be like having a normal X-ray, but the experience is different. You are immobilized under this machine, and you hear it wind up and start to irradiate. But then it keeps on going for thirty to forty seconds. That sequence was repeated from three different angles. I felt nothing in my leg, but when I asked the technicians if we start killing cancer cells from day one, they said yes. They implied that the strength of the radiation would be building over time. I don't know if they meant it is cumulative or that the actual dose will increase. I actually think the latter.

I examined my leg when I got home. And I don't glow in the dark, and I don't have a suntan yet (something I was told I would get).

Erica is cooking us dinner tonight, pork loin baked in a large casserole dish with apricots, prunes, sweet potatoes, a cup of bourbon, and served with mashed potatoes and snap beans. It is a recipe I learned at a hunting camp many years ago—  delicious, hearty, and very flexible. For every ingredient you don't happen to have at home, you just add another cup of bourbon. Keeps you regular too.

Erica flies off into America's wasteland tomorrow and returns to my grandchildren, Nicolas and Lara. I have hopes of seeing them in mid to late July. By then I should be hobbling around on crutches, but the kids should be able to enjoy the backyard swimming pool once I get it opened up. I may be calling some of you on this website to get this task completed.

Thank you for stopping by. See you tomorrow.

WRITTEN MARCH 16, 2010, 8:18 P.M.

My daughter, Erica, flew back to Minneapolis at noon today, and we just got word that she made it back safely and has picked up her kids. She was a great comfort to us while she was here. I hate it when sons and daughters move so far away from the "old folks." Yes, her husband got the big job, but what is the real emotional cost of family separation? I am on the record as endorsing how the Italian families in Middletown have grandma on the first floor and Aunt Rose on the third.

Day two of twenty-eight days of radiation went by uneventfully except for the weigh-in. I am gaining weight on all of the fine food we are eating, some from friends, some from home, and some from restaurants. Went to "East Side," the German restaurant in New Britain today. I have to work on losing a lot of weight if I am going to be navigating on less than a complete left leg in ten weeks or so.

Tuesdays are doctor days at the cancer center. We met with the head of radiology with some questions I had from reading some website articles on malignant fibrous histiocytoma (MFH). Our Dr. G suggested that I disregard everything I find on the web about MFH. He suggested that the incentive behind many of the articles is marketing for a service, a treatment plan, or a drug. He did give me one website that he felt was fairly accurate, and I will be reading everything on that site ASAP. I was inquiring about "buying an insurance policy" by having chemotherapy in addition to everything we are already doing. He thinks it's a bad idea for lots of good reasons, which I won't go into here, but if you ever want to know, give me a call. Dr. G showed us a computer-drawn picture of my tumor. It is about the size of a chicken's egg with one flat side where it pushes against muscle and bone. He says that he has dealt with much larger tumors, which makes us feel a little better.

Cindy and I want to thank everyone who is keeping up with us on this journey. Many thanks also to those who have left such encouraging messages.

Written March 17, 2010, 7:48 p.m.

First off, I want to tell you all that I really, really enjoy the guestbook entries. Knowing that friends are stopping by and leaving messages helps to keep this guy "singing in the rain." I wish that I could easily respond to the guestbook entries, but that service is not available. I have written to CaringBridge with the suggestion, but

I have not heard back from them. I plan to print them all out at some point and carefully answer where appropriate.

Bennett, I bought a new pair of lounging pants that I will be using both at the cancer center and also at your sixth birthday party on May 16th. They are "superhero pants," and all of Marvel Comics superheroes are on them. The cancer center staff is looking forward to seeing them, as I have been colorful with my choices so far, but these are quite outrageous.

Day three of twenty-eight days of radiation, and all is well. I got a tiny itch when they were irradiating my leg from the top today. I don't know if the itch was related to the radiation or not. I will be monitoring the situation and let you know. Debbie and Cindy went with me today, and they stopped off to purchase the makings of a grand spaghetti dinner, salad, homemade meatballs, pork chops, and South End Market bread (really good). (There goes my diet for today.) Last night, Kim provided a memorable dinner for us— stuffed red peppers, macaroni and cheese, squash, bread, chicken wings, followed by cannoli for desert. Delicious! Thank you. Pam has been spoiling us with food, and the other night, she stopped over with funny videos for us to enjoy. I truly feel as though I have a dozen or more friends next to me every step of the way.

We got to the cancer center early and worked on a thousand-piece jigsaw puzzle until they were able to take me. The girls got seven pieces working together. Cindy got nine pieces yesterday. I think Debbie and Cindy were gabbing instead of working the puzzle. The cancer center at the Hospital of Central Connecticut in New Britain is in a separate building behind the hospital itself. There is a private drive and parking for the "cancer center only," so it is really accessible. There is a large community room out front that has two library sitting areas, several sofas and chairs, a desktop computer for patient use, etc. It is very comfortable. About ten minutes before my appointment time, I stroll through the doors and into the main part of the building, where there is another waiting room and TV with three small changing rooms with lockers. I can pick from a large selection of Johnnies or wear my own baggy clothes, which is what I generally do. They usually come for me within ten minutes of my appointment time, and it's a short walk to the treatment room. As I mentioned before, treatment only takes a few minutes after they have me locked into the leg jigs on the table.

I continue to be happy with the hospital, cancer center, doctors, and technicians. Couple that with all your support, and I really feel very blessed.

WRITTEN MARCH 18, 2010, 12:20 P.M.

Special Journal Entry

This morning after my coffee, I sat down to read any new guestbook entries that came in overnight.

Honestly, I was overwhelmed to see the below message from Ralph Thompson. Yes, I did shed a tear or two. Ralph is a missionary in Kenya who is supported by my home church, Fellowship Church, Saybrook Road, Middletown (www.fellowshipchurchct.com).

Ralph grew up in our church. He is one of us. I met Ralph, his wife, Sandy, and their children some years ago while Ralph was still working toward completing all of the preparation that needs to be done before establishing a missionary work in a foreign country. I didn't understand Ralph then, and I don't understand him now. I am just not able to understand the love that someone has for others and for his God, which would allow them to move everything precious to them (the whole family) to an African country to work among the poor and the unchurched. His family went. They had more children there in that country, and they have all fought malaria and other sicknesses that just don't show up here. Ralph is doing something way bigger than most of us could imagine doing, and yet he has time to send me greetings and encouragement. Ralph, I am embarrassed to gratefully accept your best wishes and especially your prayers. I am praying Romans 8:28, surrendering to God's love and His wishes for my life. I consider myself in a win-win situation here, and I just want to share my experiences with my friends. Ralph, I will be looking up your web address and find out how someone can begin following your work. You cannot begin to appreciate how important your message was to me.

Yours in Christ,
Bob Schulte

Ralph's Message to Me

Hi, Bob,

It has been great to read the journal entries and different posts in the guestbook. I can see God is using many people to demonstrate his love for you through encouragement, humor, and offers for help. What a blessing! You're strength and faith are very evident and inspiring. Know that we are also cheering you on, albeit from the other side of the globe. You will definitely be in our thoughts and prayers. Looking forward to connecting with you this summer.

Ralph Thompson
Mombassa
Kenya

Written March 18, 2010, 9:51 p.m.

Day four of twenty-eight done. I actually worked a couple of hours today on a computer job in Madison and will be working at town hall tomorrow. My leg feels better now than before the radiation began. I don't know if the cancer is shrinking or just has stopped growing, either way is okay with me.

My superhero pants were a big hit today at the cancer center, and the radiation therapists said I could bring my camera in tomorrow and take some pictures of the equipment we are using. They have a great attitude about the work they are doing, and they love their jobs. Jimmy, one of the therapists, is up in Rhode Island at the NCAA games. He will be there for three games.

Cindy and I are thinking more about dieting. Will thinking about it help?

WRITTEN MARCH 19, 2010, 8:09 P.M.

Day five of twenty-eight, the first week is done!

Hello, all,

I am tired tonight as I had a busy day. I haven't visited my office in Durham Town Hall, (I am registrar of voters for Durham) for at least four weeks, and my Democratic counterpart has been shouldering the burden. Karen did a great job. Thank you very much.

Karen and I are preparing for a county meeting of registrars next week. We call ourselves cochairs. But really, Karen is the chairman, and I am the assistant. We are in our second term and still having fun. We alternate going to the monthly state meetings. The Semi-Annual Connecticut State ROVAC Convention is on April 22nd and 23rd. I hope to be able to audit several of the morning classes, but radiation is finishing up for me around then, so I may not feel up to it.

It is another sunny day with temps hovering around 70 degrees. The cancer center is on top of Walnut Hill in New Britain. It has a commanding view to the southeast toward Meriden and New Haven. There is a nice garden out front with a short walkway through it and a couple of park benches. When we are early, we sit outside on the benches. It is very relaxing. The garden is looking hopeful—little shoots of green in some of the larger cut-down shrubs. A couple of chrysanthemums wintered well and are starting to grow, and there are red buds on some of the ornamental trees. I guess I will get to see what they all become.

The radiation session was normal except for my taking some pictures. This laboratory is really cool with all the dials and switches. All that is missing are a couple of Van de Graff generators, and we'd have the makings of the next *Frankenstein* movie.

Written March 22, 2010, 4:37 p.m.

Day six of twenty-eight.

Back to radiation after a weekend off. The weather has been great until today. We had fog in the hills around us this morning and a dreary, rainy day. Temps only in the low fifties, I think.

I found that I am a lot braver when Cindy is around. She had a few commitments yesterday and today, and I became pretty blah when she was away. I hadn't realized how she lit up my life before. I guess it is a good thing to find that out about someone. I knew she was my rock, but I did not know I would react like that to her absence. I'd better be good so that she sticks it out with me. LOL

Cindy was watching the grandkids as they both have strep throat per the doctor's orders. Deb rode up with me today, and I got to drive her new vehicle. It is a Volkswagen "something" AWD. Very nice to drive and solid on the road.

The radiation therapists are great folks, and Jim is an avid basketball fan, so I enjoyed the banter back and forth. How about those UConn women, ninety-five to thirty-nine over Southern this weekend. How long can that go on?

The radiation treatment was the same as usual. I didn't feel a thing when they were doing it today.

WRITTEN MARCH 23, 2010, 5:46 P.M.

Day seven of twenty-eight.

Today's treatment included some quality assurance work. After I was set up in the jig, the therapists took two sets of four X-rays, each to see if the leg bones and jig still agreed with the original settings. They made adjustments and repainted some targets that are set up on my leg. They told me that they work in the millimeter range, which is pretty amazing when you think about shooting rays into the human body.

It's Tuesday, so I was weighed and had a meeting with the doctor after the radiation. (Donna, no change in weight yet. I must confess I had ice cream last night.)

Hey, that reminds me. I would like to practice walking with crutches. If anyone has a pair that would work for a tall adult like me, I would like to borrow them. The surgeon told me that they will not let me come home from the hospital until I can handle fourteen stairs on crutches. My operation won't happen until around May 30th, but practice may be helpful now and reduce any time I may have to put in at a rehab center.

I got to sit with Dr. G again today, and I asked him what to expect from this radiation treatment. He said that the swelling on my leg will not go down until about five to seven weeks after the radiation treatments end ... or just about the time I go in for surgery. He said that I should expect some tiredness in a couple of weeks, and a red sore leg as well. He said that I needed to be able to deal with the possibility that the radiation may need to be suspended for a couple of weeks to allow my leg to heal before we finish the radiation regimen. I am glad that I am being told these things, but it is a bit maddening to have so many delays in the treatment process. Special thanks to Pam for all the attention I am getting, to Debbie for driving on Mondays, and to Mary for the food and driving offers, and to my kids for their constant attention and well-wishes. Donna, thanks for the banter in the guestbook. Nancy, I enjoyed our conversation today and would love and appreciate the opportunity to give you a guided tour of Fellowship Church.

It is one of the best kept secrets in Middletown, and I am bound and determined to change that.

All in all, life is good. Thank you all, and God bless.

WRITTEN MARCH 24, 2010, 7:20 P.M.

Day eight of twenty-eight.

I wanted to share with you a surprise I had this afternoon during my radiation treatments. The treatment itself was done, and I was getting set to head back to the changing room. I was chatting with the therapists and looking over the equipment in the room when one of them asked if I would like to see more. "Yes, indeed," I answered. She then took me to the little hallway that separated the treatment room from the rest of the facility and said, "Let me show you our door." I looked around and saw what looked like it might be a sliding door that would close off the hallway, but that was not it. She asked me to stand clear, and she pushed a big red button under a sign that said, "Danger: High Radiation." When she pushed the button, a solid steel door that was twenty inches thick came across the little hallway and sealed off the treatment room. It was like a bank vault door without the locking bars. I must tell you that with my touch of claustrophobia, I never again will feel quite so comfortable during the treatment process after I saw that door. On the other hand, in case of nuclear attack, I would be all set.

Then she led me into the control room located across the hall. It was a round room about twenty-five feet in diameter, and there were computer monitors and video screens all over the walls. I counted fourteen workstations, but they said that only one half were manned at any one time as the rest controlled a different room used for CT scans. They never ran both rooms at the same time as the same people ran both rooms, and the team was only large enough to operate one room at a time. They showed me camera feeds of the treatment room, set up so they could watch every move the patient made. As I mentioned in an earlier journal entry, they are very meticulous about setting the treatment up so that the radiation hits just the right spot. Even today, they took more X-rays to be sure of my alignment.

The conversation turned to computers, and I told them about my small company "Computer House Call." Before it was over, I had one of the therapists bringing her personal laptop in to me tomorrow for repair!

WRITTEN MARCH 26, 2010, 12:18 A.M.

Day nine of twenty-eight.

Today was busy, fun, and exhausting. It is after midnight, and this journal entry has taken me too long. I know I have run on a bit, but there is so much to tell you.

My little sister, Ann, and two of her grown-up sons visited today on their way to Boston. She is a Montessori teacher in Glen Spey, NY, and has a conference or workshop in bean town this weekend. It was a pleasant, unannounced surprise. I don't hear from my sister very often, but then she didn't hear from me often either. I would like to work together toward changing that. Mom, would be happy. I love you, Ann.

I continue to receive way more attention then even I can comfortably handle. I confess that during my unchurched years, I was always happy to take a bow or accept the credit. After all, without God, isn't that what life is all about? The guy with the big job and the most toys wins!

Amazingly, I have "prayer warriors" on three continents that I know of, all praying for me, and today, I received a call from

Wesleyan University that the entire Christian fellowship (WESCF) has been notified and they are all praying as well. When I chat with God, I almost feel like I should apologize for the time He must be spending listening to you guys. We are all magnificently blessed that we have such a friend in Jesus. Please know, all of you, that I am fine. I trust in the Lord and have no fear for my future. I am forever changed by the outpouring of love that I have felt since this blessing came upon me. My prayer for you is that in your own time of need, you may share in the comfort that God has given me at this time. My train, #97, has steamed up and is running on wonderful tracks of shining steel, fired by Grace. The only thing I don't know is where the final stop will be, but then none of you know either. Friends, we are all passengers. Our Engineer is the way, the truth, and the light. Hang on to that, and we will all be okay.

Treatment today was as normal as being bombarded with radiation can be. I have tried to learn something new each day, and today, I learned about the "on-board imager" OBI system incorporated in the particle accelerator used in New Britain.

Up until this generation of linear accelerators, radiation oncologists have had to contend with variations in patient positioning and with respiratory motion by treating a margin of healthy tissue around the tumor. IGRT allows doctors to locate the tumor using high-resolution X-ray or CT-scan images while the patient is in the treatment position and minimize the exposure of healthy tissue during the radiation treatment.

The doctor's software package allows him to construct the tumor in 3-D using the CT scan, PET scan, and X-ray as data sets. The image of the 3-D tumor is used by a physicist to program the accelerator much like a CNC machine can work on a block of steel to fashion a finished part after multiple operations. The radiation head moves around the target (me) and adjusts itself to the movement of the tumor in order to minimize collateral damage.

I continue to be impressed with the people, their attitudes, the equipment, and the facilities at New Britain General Hospital of Central Connecticut. If there are any LP'ers (living proof is our fellowship for teens) out there reading this, people who are searching for career opportunities, the field of radiation therapist looks pretty good to me. Every therapist I have met is very conscientious and seems to understand just how important their skills are, both physically and mentally.

WRITTEN MARCH 26, 2010, 10:42 P.M.

Day ten of twenty-eight

Today was a day of no surprises. Radiation therapy went quickly, and my leg after two weeks of radiation is just showing a little pink on top of the tumor. Several weeks ago when we were in Canada, the cancer was growing very fast. I had mild discomfort walking and occasional jabs of pain when I moved my leg one way or the other or when I hit it on a hard object. (I should pause and tell you that once you have a tender spot on your leg, it is impossible to make water at night without hitting the thing on the side of the bed or in our case, a large chest at the foot of the bed that Cindy keeps all of her treasures in.) Anyway, I have no discomfort at all now, and the suggestion of weakness in the leg that I had last week was unfounded. It is as strong as ever now. I think that the radiation must be doing some good internally. The doctor said that in the lower leg, there are a bunch of muscles that control your toes and that they all were getting pretty squeezed by my tumor.

Debbie, Cindy, and I attended the Filipino Cultural Celebration Dinner at Wesleyan this evening and got to see several of the Wesleyan Christian Fellowship (WESCF) students who were a part of the evening's performances. We ate suckling pig, chop suey, flan, and several other main dishes. There also was a *Fear Factor* competition, and contestants had to eat several rather frightening items. The worst one was an egg consisting of the partially grown embryo with feathers and a beak. You break off the top of the egg/embryo and drink the clear liquid on top and then peel the egg and take it down in two large bites. It is very meaty and chewy, yet I am told it still tastes like a boiled egg. I did not try that, but I did eat bits of fish skin that was deep fried with spicy additives. Usually eaten with rice, it wasn't bad. I left the chicken's feet and the pork blood stew alone.

It was really great to see the non-Filipino Wesleyan students trying to dance the ethnic Filipino dances, and enjoying the main courses. Everyone enjoyed the evening and came away with a greater appreciation of the Filipino way of life.

Off to bed now, and a small computer job at 8:00 a.m. tomorrow morning. Then lunch at Cindy's parents. Good night, John Boy.

WRITTEN MARCH 28, 2010, 6:25 P.M.

The weekend.

A fairly quiet weekend. We visited Cindy's parents down in Haddam and enjoyed a simple lunch with them. Cindy's nephew, Clayton, and his two kids stopped by to make a delivery. Twenty-four dollars and six boxes of Girl Scout cookies later, they left, and we got down to serious chatting, snoozing, and a little bit computer repair. We got home in time to start our income taxes on the computer but not in time to see Matt's new toy. It was off to bed reasonably early.

Sunday was a slow day for us as well. We enjoyed Andy's sermon very much and leftovers of Andrew's grandma's eightieth birthday cake. It was good! Thank you, Donna and Dave, for the loan of the crutches. I like them as they appear to be an older pair and have a certain patina in the stained wood finish. I will be practicing stairs after I set them up for my size.

I hope your weekend was good as well. Tomorrow starts the third week of radiation, day number eleven of twenty-eight.

Written March 29, 2010, 5:27 p.m.

Day eleven of twenty-eight.

Rain again—only this time, I know why! The Coleman Carnival is setting up in Middletown! I don't know what it is with that bunch, but whatever weekend they come into town, it rains. My guess is that eight out of the last ten years, it has happened that way.

On Mondays, Cindy provides childcare for Sadie, so either I go alone or Debbie goes with me. It takes my mind off of the whole procedure when I have a friend with me. New Britain is one good conversation up and another back. It just works out that way. On the way up, we talked about Andy and some of that stuff was good. On the way back, we talked about Marie, one of the cancer patients I see every day. Let me explain. The way it works is that the staff at the cancer center schedules patients on what looks to me to be about a twenty-minute cycle, so three different people got through treatment each hour. The treatments take almost no time at all. In my case, three minutes. Most of the time is used during the setup phase. As I mentioned in previous journal entries, the therapists bend over backward to get the patient into exactly the correct position so that collateral damage is minimized.

Anyway, the way it works is that each patient meets the person before next and the patient after him or her stays in the waiting room. Everyone gets to sit and joke about the "johnnies" that are provided, or in my case, the superhero pants that I wear. I have only been there for two weeks but already have formed interesting friendships with my fellow cancer patients, in particular with Marie. Marie is a woman of about seventy who is in great shape otherwise but who has cervical cancer and has had the full regimen of chemo and radiation thrown at her. She only noticed the problem as spotting that started six weeks ago. It was a whirlwind rush of doctor appointments, and then treatment began. She has been through five rounds of chemo and has been really sick with it the whole time. The chemo was so bad that she has been coming into the hospital two to three days a week for hydration therapy. She has not been able to drink anything for a long time. She was so happy today because yesterday, she was able to drink eight ounces of ginger ale down without throwing it up. Anyway, we were chatting in a way that perhaps only cancer patients can. We talked about our lives. I know all about her wonderful daughter who took her in for the duration (she is a widow), and she has met Cindy in the outer waiting room and chatted with her. Her daughter must have a very big house, as Marie is staying in the "bird room" after the birds were all moved out to the enclosed sunroom. She said her daughter had the bird room redone for her. Anyway, all of the above to tell you this: Last Friday was a particularly difficult day for Marie. She had a chemo appointment for 11:30 a.m., and her everyday radiation appointment at 2:40 p.m. She got to the hospital on time; however, they were running behind, and she did not get to go into the intravenous room until 12:45 p.m. Her next problem was that they could not find a vein even after a good number of attempts. She then had to wait for another hour until a senior nurse could come down and get the intravenous needle started. By then it was 3:00 p.m. So she missed her appointment time for radiation in the cancer center next door. The chemo center closed at 4:00 p.m., and she was whisked over in a wheelchair to the cancer center for her radiation. Well, Marie, who considers herself a very strong individual, found out just how much she could take and broke down sobbing in the wheelchair in the hallway of the radiation building. She told me that the therapists surrounded her wheelchair and told her to just let it all come out—all the fear, all the frustration, all the sorrow—and they comforted her for twenty minutes before her radiation treatment. Maybe none of what I am saying touches you like it is hitting me, but I was almost in tears with this woman. If you know someone with cancer, reach out to them, offer to go with them to treatments, just let them vent to you. Marie told me that she has never cried about her cancer in front of her family or friends. She wants so badly to be brave. I was touched that she would drop her guard and tell me the story. I am so happy that she felt safe enough in the cancer center to have herself a good cry. She said the therapists were absolutely wonderful through the whole thing, and she said that after her radiation treatment, it was as if a weight had been lifted off of her and she was ready again to continue the fight. Please pray with me for Marie. I am grateful that she told me her story.

WRITTEN MARCH 30, 2010, 6:29 P.M.

Day twelve of twenty-eight.

Not much to report today. Radiation therapy went normally but a little late. Tuesday is weigh-in and doctor visit after treatment. He reports I have a slight erythema in the skin around the tumor. It is slightly red, and the capillaries have swollen. It is nothing serious and common in areas of skin that have received more than two gray units of radiation. My full treatment is over fifty gray units, and I am twelve days into a twenty-eight-day regimen, so I am over two units but have not done the math.

I like rainy days. (How can you appreciate the sun if you don't have rain?) But I feel quite tired today. I haven't decided if I am just being lazy or if I'm beginning to feel the fatigue that goes along with radiation in many people. More on this as we go on.

I want to spend some time this week thinking, reading, and praying about *The Passion*, which is remembered this weekend. Cindy just told me that Tyson gave us a copy of the movie *The Passion*, so we will plan on seeing it this week. If someone would like to borrow it for Saturday, please call us. First come, first serve.

See you all tomorrow.

WRITTEN MARCH 31, 2010, 9:19 P.M.

Day thirteen of twenty-eight

Not too much to report today. Radiation went smoothly as it does every day. I was in at 2:45 and out by 3:30.

We got into the New Britain area a little earlier than usual, so we did some riding around, looking at the big three-family houses. New Britain was called "the Hardware Capital of the World" for very good reason. It was/is the home of Fafnir Bearing, General Appliances, the Stanley Works, which included Stanley Tools, Stanley Hardware, and Stanley Steel Strapping. Corbin Lock made its home there as did New Britain Tools, Russwin Locks, and others. Machinists from all over the world emigrated to New Britain, and strong German and Polish ethnic groups and clubs still exist there. The large multifamily homes were built to support the thousands of blue-collar workers that called New Britain home. My own history with Stanley Tools began in 1968, which was probably ten years after the apex for New Britain. Business continued to flourish there, but more and more product was being sourced from overseas. First, it was Germany and Spain, and then it came from the Asian nations, starting with Japan.

Today, almost all of the companies I mentioned no longer have plants in New Britain. The thousand of homes and apartments emptied of worker families and minorities moved into the cheap rents that became available. New Britain's downtown includes many shuttered buildings and certainly is not an inviting shopping area any longer.

My therapists today reviewed with me some of the things that are done to ensure quality. Every morning at 7:30, a specially trained technician puts the Varian 2100 EX through its paces and measures the doses of radiation that it puts out for accuracy to instrumentation. Daily, the therapists run a test to ensure the same thing, and weekly, the physicist in charge of the whole operation reviews each patient's records and makes any adjustments necessary.

I am very sure that I have made the right move to go to New Britain for treatment.

WRITTEN APRIL 1, 2010, 6:05 P.M.

Fourteen of twenty-eight—*halfway!*

Food for Thought

Here's some advice: When you chat with a cancer patient and are saying good-bye, don't say, "Take care. I know everything will be all right." My dermatologist did just that today—a real disappointment.

Today started out gray with a chill that reminded us of winter yet still allowed for spring. It started at 50 degrees early, but by midafternoon, it was 68 degrees. All in all, a very nice and sunny day. There is a cherry tree outside the cancer center, and it is turning red and getting ready to bloom. Tiny leaves are coming out, and the buds are forming. It will take another two weeks perhaps. I will let you know.

Cindy, who follows me in radiation at 3:20, was there as well as Cliff, someone who follows Cindy. He is about sixty-five or so and came in with a motorcycle helmet on. He rode his BMW R69S, which he bought new in 1972. We chatted, and I asked him where his cancer was. He said that he had prostate cancer but that it is no longer there. It was kind of a lighthearted comment, but he stunned me by saying that now it had traveled throughout his body and he was being treated with chemotherapy and full-body radiation. We chatted a little while longer, and then I left kind of shell-shocked. When I left, I promised Cliff and Cindy that I would place them on my prayer list. And I wished them a happy Easter. I ask that all believers that read this do the same and ask all nonbelievers to consider your mortality. Do you really think that the beauty and complexity you see around you and the miracle of life that you shared with God in your children could be some Darwinian coincidence?

WRITTEN APRIL 2, 2010, 4:12 P.M.

Day fifteen of twenty-eight.

My radiation treatment time got switched to 9:00 a.m. today so that the therapists could start their Easter weekend a little early. We were up by 7:00 with the alarm clock and out the door by about 7:55 so we could make a deposit at the dump on the way. (Actually, a friend's dumpster, as we forgot to go to the dump yesterday.) It is a beautiful sunny day, and now even the rosebushes at the cancer center are showing a little growth on their short, cut-back branches. I have never had any luck with roses. My hat is off to those of you who have.

The treatment was fast, and I met a couple of strangers who were there for treatment because of the rearranged schedule. The talk was stunted. I definitely am looking to go back into the queue where I belong at 3:00 p.m. It is strange how comfort levels develop.

After the treatment, we took Cindy's car for its state mandated emissions test, and aside from dealing with terrible customer service, everything worked out fine. And apparently, the global climate control cops will be leaving us alone for the time being.

When we got home, I made crepes for lunch. Afterward, I felt very tired, so I lay down and promptly slept for almost four hours. I was really exhausted but felt better as a result. Now it's back to business and getting ready for our Good Friday service at church.

I think that some of the exhaustion that I felt may be from the radiation as I was light-headed along with the fatigue and swooned once or twice before I lay down. Anyway, I am glad that is over for today.

WRITTEN APRIL 3, 2010, 12:48 P.M.

Just a quick note: I am bright-eyed and bushy-tailed again today. I don't know what happened yesterday with the light-headedness and fatigue, but it is not here now.

Last night, we had our Good Friday service and had a great time with all of our teens attending with the adult members and guests. We had a drama skit and a group activity as a part of the service, but my favorite moment was when Debbie sang the "Via Della Rosa" while a video short depicted Christ on the way to Calvary. As an aside, Debbie had a nice group of family members with her for the service, and lo and behold, her sister, Cindy, was there, who is also the Cindy that takes her radiation just after me! It's a small world after all!

It is almost a contradiction to feel this good about such a terrible event (*The Passion*) in history, but it is that seminal event that made it possible for us to stand before our creator at judgment time, knowing that there is a place for us in heaven. Thank you, Jesus, for the work that you did not have to do but chose to do for us. You took the full weight of all sin upon your shoulders and made our salvation possible.

So tomorrow is my sixteenth out of twenty-eight days of radiation. I thank God every day for the peace and tranquility that he has provided me at this time. I am also thanking God that Sadie and Bennett will be spending about four and a half days with us when Bennett's school is closed for vacation. The men, Bennett and I, and maybe Rich, if he can make it, plan on drowning some worms in Phyllis's farm pond. We hope to fish at least two or three times.

Afterward, it's a man's shore lunch we will be doing. Fish and toasted marshmallows—*I can't wait!*

WRITTEN APRIL 5, 2010, 5:17 P.M.

Day sixteen of twenty-eight.

After radiation today, they wanted another blood test: complete blood count (CBC). Radiation can have an effect on your blood, and they check it for changes.

"With radiation therapy, the side effects depend on the treatment dose and the part of the body that is treated. The most common side effects are tiredness, skin reactions (such as a rash or redness, permanent pigmentation, and scarring) in the treated area, and loss of appetite (I wish!). Radiation therapy can cause inflammation of tissues and organs in and around the body site radiated. This can cause symptoms that depend on what organs are affected and to what degree. For example, radiation can inflame skin to cause a burn or permanent pigmentation. Radiation therapy can also cause a decrease in the number of white blood cells, cells that help protect the body against infection." So I guess they are counting white blood cells.

WRITTEN APRIL 6, 2010, 7:02 P.M.

Day seventeen of twenty-eight.

Another great date with the Varians 2100EX. (See photo section.) Radiation is going well. As a matter of fact, my leg looks as if it is done to at least medium. The day was really busy. I am about four hours from being done with my income taxes, but I just don't feel like doing it tonight. I worked for about four and a half hours today on computer jobs, and then there was the radiation, which is tiring because it's almost an hour each way by the time you drive to New Britain and get there fifteen minutes early. On the way home, we stopped for an early dinner pizza at DaVinci's in

Rockfall, and I had to rush to get to a client's home for 5:00. Dr. G thinks it is going well, and he (the radiologist) is optimistic about the surgery. He is assuring me that the surgeon, Dr F, has done far larger tumors than mine.

I was fooling around with the website and added a couple of pictures. I am very proud of the one with Bennett and Opa reading the Marvel comic book. I read the first half to Bennett, and he read the second half to me. Bennett is in kindergarten I couldn't read superhero comic books until third grade. My three other grandchildren are also doing extremely well. We are so fortunate to have been blessed with healthy, well-adjusted grandkids.

Duke beat Baylor by the narrowest of margins last night. I hope UConn's women have another good game tonight. They deserve the national championship after they've run seventy-seven games in a row without a loss. Red Sox beat the Yankees in the opener on Sunday. All is good in my house tonight. Hope the Sox do it again tonight.

The only thing I have on my mind now is getting the last of the siding done on the house. Volunteers needed. Marcel? Bill? Mark? Allan? Anyone?

WRITTEN APRIL 7, 2010, 9:17 P.M.

Day eight of twenty-eight.

I bet you guys are as bored with my repetitive radiation treatments as I am! I can tell you this: If it weren't for the professionalism I see every day with the "crew" and the really nice facility that I am being treated in, I would be going nuts by now. The leg is now officially *red* and sensitive to the touch over the tumor, not painfully sensitive, just sensitive like a mild sunburn would be. The doctor thinks my leg is handling the radiation well, and yesterday, he showed us the way he was attacking the tumor with radiation. (Tuesday is weigh-in and doctor day.) In cross-section, the tumor is five-sided with a couple of the sides being rounded. He explained that he designed the angle of treatment and the dosage to preserve as much tissue as possible around the tumor. He is really very optimistic about the future success of the surgery.

I am kind of taking this thing one day at a time, as it is dealt. I can't explain it. I don't want to start being overly optimistic as I don't want to have to start over in dealing with it if something goes wrong. At one point when they thought I had cancer in my lungs, I thought the worst. I have not really allowed myself to come all the way back from that position. Don't ask me to explain it, but I don't want to deal with major disappointment. If I work hard to accept the worst, then everything else is really good.

So Dr. G found out I was a licensed captain, and we talked boats. He has a house on the Connecticut River on the Essex/Deep River line. He has his own dock that needs some repair, but he does not have a boat right now. He is interested in something like an Albin 28 or Mainship 30 used. I think he really likes his toys. His two cars are a BMW M6 and a new Range Rover. Something over five hundred horsepower and zero-to-sixty times of 4.8 seconds. He also has a girlfriend as opposed to a wife and wears colored socks. Always a warning as you know.

By the way, the flowering tree is a pink cherry tree, and it is in full bloom. The ground plants are coming, but it is too soon to say exactly what they are, although I think there may be some clump grasses coming up. The leaves are about three inches long right now and very thin. I will be taking some pictures for you tomorrow.

Written April 9, 2010, 8:48 p.m.

Days nineteen and twenty of twenty-eight.

I am a little vexed today. I labored through a rough draft of a journal entry and then left the computer to work on my income tax. When I came back, the program had thrown me out because of a lack of activity. I hate that some of my best material was lost. Now you will have to contend with a hastily written but truthful account instead of my PC version.

Days nineteen (yesterday) and twenty (today) went very smoothly as always. My leg is definitely weaker than it was when we started, with the biggest item of notice being a lack of control when I stride forward with the left leg while I'm walking. You can hear my left shoe slapping down onto the floor at times. It feels less secure than my right foot. This is probably a result of the radiation damage to the whole leg. I hope that this repairs itself during the five-to-eight interim weeks before surgery.

We had some excitement with Cindy as well this week. I took her to the doctor because of a swelling that she has on her left jaw just under the ear. As it turned out, the doctor said she was too sweet and prescribed sour balls and antibiotics—the antibiotics to fight the infection in her salivary gland and the sour balls to make her salivate a lot. The worry here is that she may develop a "stone" in the gland, which is troublesome to fix.

WRITTEN APRIL 11, 2010, 6:56 P.M.

In a faraway land beyond the rivers and the Great Plains, lives my granddaughter, Lara, in the "land of lakes." Lara lives near the Minnehaha Creek, where it empties into the mighty Mississippi.

Far from the lands of her OPA, she labors with her studies and fights mighty battles in order to be prepared for the marvels that await her in life.

In the eighth year of her life, she was challenged by her school oracle to enter a "third dimension" and travel to distant lands in her new form.

She became "Flat Lara," made of paper, and with Crayola colors, she was challenged to travel far and wide and document her lingerings along the way. Notes and photos and other news of her travels would ultimately be shared with other members of her warren.

Flat Lara traveled east, far east into the land of Schulte beyond the Great Hudson, into the state of Constitution and the Kingdom of Durham.

It was there that she spied her OPA awaiting her arrival and bidding her welcome.

Flat Lara traveled to Quebec City in the Canadian lands last month and travels with OPA now as he is treated at the hospital in New Britain.

Look carefully in the photo section. You will see Flat Lara during her travels. She helped Meme with the jigsaw puzzle in the cancer center and inspected the credentials of the therapist. She even cheered up Cindi as she waited for her treatment.

Flat Lara has been a great help to OPA and will be returning home soon. She will carry with her all the memories of her travels, and she will be much missed, but not nearly as much as Lara herself. I love you, Lara!

WRITTEN APRIL 12, 2010, 7:00 P.M.

Day twenty-one of twenty-eight.

Holy smokes! I broke it! I broke a 1.4-million-dollar machine … or at least that is what I thought today when the Varian 2100 EX would not rotate correctly. We (or really they) started trying everything to make it rotate. I suggested they "reboot it" and received a couple of snickers in return. A breakdown like that would literally shut down their operation at great cost. After a couple of minutes of screwing with the controls, someone checked the remote control (looks like a TV remote) and found the batteries were dead. Woo-hoo! Back in business, and my "tanning session" continues.

Strange that I will miss these people when I am done. We have had a lot of laughs, and their professionalism is very comforting. Does anyone know what kind of gift to give a mixed gender team of radiation therapists? I mean really?

I am able to see that my movement and feeling is affected now by the accumulating radiation. It is ever-so-little, but I am dragging the foot and losing some movement and feeling in the toes. Not a big deal. I must look funny, stumbling around like a drunken sailor. My mom used to call my father a drunken sailor, but for a somewhat better reason.

Thank you, all who appreciated the "Flat Lara" narrative. It actually was fun playing with the words and trying to harken back to the times of yore. My daughter, Erica, thinks that I would have made a very pretty eight-year-old, very happy.

Cindy and I are licensed grandparents and have four grandchildren. They are my daughter Erica's children, Nicolas (Cole) and Lara, and Cindy's daughter Vicki's children, Bennett and Sadie. Each one brings us great joy. Would that they could stay this age forever?

It seems as if it is our turn to exercise the health-care system. Cindy and I were helping Vicki with our two grandchildren today.

(School is off this week.) And Bennett started to complain about a pain in his belly. It got progressively worse. He developed a fever of 101.7, and by lunchtime, Bennett didn't even want to go to McDonald's for lunch. Something was obviously wrong. A 2:15 doctor's appointment, and we are watching him now for possible appendicitis. Go figure.

Late breaking news, Bennett seems fine, and we will have him again tomorrow—campfire, marshmallows, and fishing. Can't wait.

WRITTEN APRIL 13, 2010, 7:17 P.M.

Day twenty-two of twenty-eight.

I am in a sour mood today as we are dealing with a couple of issues that have managed to get my goat. For starters, I can no longer control my toes or lift them while I'm standing. I stand there and strain, and nothing happens. It kind of feels like a cramp when I try hard. The result is that the foot tends to hang when I am in stride so that the sole of my shoe drags as I move it forward while I'm walking. I have stumbled a couple of times. Much more of this, and I will be using a cane.

The leg also is slowly going numb from the cancer down to the foot. There is now a constant discomfort, not a pain that I can complain about but a feeling like you get when you sit in one position for a long time and you have to straighten out your leg and work it to get comfortable. (Perhaps if you are under fifty years old, you have never felt this.) The radiation has also burned the leg, and the doctor seemed surprised that I wasn't complaining. I don't feel particularly brave about this. It is what it is, but the leg is getting ugly now. The doctor said that I should continue the radiation to completion (six more days) but that he wanted to consult with my surgeon over the loss of feeling and loss of toe control. He said that should not have happened.

On the way home, I got a phone call from the radiologist's office, one telling me that he had reached Dr. F, the surgeon, and that Dr. F wanted to see me. I immediately called Dr. F for an appointment and was told he didn't have any time available until April 26th. When I told the nurse/receptionist that I was calling because Dr. F wanted to see me, she got all huffy as if I didn't understand her. I asked her to speak to Dr. F and ask him if he wanted to see me this week. She reluctantly agreed and said she would call me back. I will be discussing this with her, and perhaps the doctor when I get to the office. I will demand better treatment from that office in the future.

On the bright side, Bennett, my grandson, has strep throat and not appendicitis. We are surprised to find out from the doctor that more than one appendix has been removed in error because of strep. There is stomach pain with strep sometimes! Go figure! Now at least we know what to do for him. He is drawing an airplane on the dining room table after he had the Colonel's popcorn chicken, which is now his favorite. Poor Vicki, but what are grandparents for anyway.

WRITTEN APRIL 14, 2010, 8:13 P.M.

Day twenty-three of twenty-eight

This is Lara, my granddaughter from Minneapolis. She drew the "Flat Lara" mentioned in an earlier journal entry. She is a strong

Schulte girl who knows what she wants and is not afraid to work hard to get it. She is a very good student and capable. Look out, world. Here she comes!

About 9:30 this morning, I received a call from Dr. F's office. They wanted to confirm an appointment with me for Friday afternoon. This call put an end to the drama that started yesterday when the woman told me I couldn't get in to see him until after April 26th—and that was after he called me to get me into the office fast. I am glad that whatever he has to say to me doesn't have to wait ten days. I will wait patiently for the opportunity to do a little critique of their customer service. Dr. F was interested in my opinion when I mentioned to him on my first visit that I knew one of the workers in his office. I had worked with her at Stanley over twenty-five years ago. He made it sound as if he was struggling to find good people. I may have found out why.

Another round of radiation is in the book, and it went well. When I got set up on the table, with my leg in the jig, the radiologists were talking about my "longitude" being off. After further inspection, they found that the baseplate pins on the jig had been inserted into the wrong set of holes on the table. Nice to know that these things are checked before the ray gun is fired. I should mention that there is always more than one technician and as many as four in the treatment room checking each other's work. Their mention of the longitude measurement was an invitation to speak to them about latitude as well. They use a system very similar to the one we use on the water to navigate. Using latitude and longitude in millimeters instead of degrees of arc allow them to measure accurately to any point under the head of the Varian 2100 EX machine. They then measure in distance to the mouth of the gun and thus can define fixed points in space. The latitude and longitude grid is projected by the Varian machine onto the subject. Finding a spot is as easy as looking at the squares on a road map but to a much finer scale.

Cindy and I have been invited to a free breakfast in honor of cancer survivors at a country club on Sunday, June 6th. We would like to go, but why must it be on a Sunday morning? Doesn't anyone go to church anymore? And while I am raving, how is it that organized school sports, such as soccer, can be scheduled for Sunday mornings? I'm done.

WRITTEN APRIL 15, 2010, 8:56 P.M.

Day twenty-four of twenty-eight.

Cindy and I arrived at the cancer center a little early, and she began working on a new jigsaw puzzle. The thousand-piece puzzle that she had been working on with unknown others was finished on last Friday. The new puzzle is only five hundred pieces; however, there is a large field of blue sky with no other colors, and the shapes will be the only hint. Difficult.

Today was supposed to be a simple radiation treatment because it's Thursday, and then there was a visit with the nurse who checks the tumor site and makes recommendations on how best to topically treat the damage. I was surprised to be told that Dr. G, the radiologist, wanted to see us. It's really easy to think unhealthy thoughts when doctors want to talk to you. This was different. He had an explanation for all of the recent conversations and concerns. He explained that when he saw that my foot was being affected the other day, he didn't know why, so he wanted Dr. F to see it. I have an appointment with Dr. F tomorrow afternoon, but both men had a discussion. Dr. F was not surprised by the foot failure as there were signs of nerve damage earlier on from the tumor. Now he knows that he will be removing the peroneal nerve among other structures in the surgery. Tomorrow's appointment with him should result in a date for surgery and a review of the "workup" that I will need to complete in preparation. Planned dates for surgery are flexible to allow for emergencies, so most surgical procedures occur one to two weeks late per Dr. G.

When you deal with people every weekday for six weeks, you develop new friendships. I will actually miss my radiation team when I am done next Wednesday; however, I know that they hope never to see me again, and that makes them professionals.

I am pleased that Dr. G took the time to explain to us why he was concerned and tell us the net result of his conversations with Dr. F. My cancer treatment group continues to encourage me.

WRITTEN APRIL 16, 2010, 8:14 P.M.

Day twenty-five of twenty-eight (five weeks done, three days of radiation left).

Before I get started reporting on today, I want to mention how wonderful the guestbook entries have been. It is pretty awesome that the website has experienced over 1,600 hits so far. Okay, so subtract a hundred or so for the times I have checked in to see what the guestbook says.

Old friends and new friends have stopped in. People I worked for and with have stopped in. Your contact through the website has helped me maintain my composure. I am not immune to fear. Sometimes I do ask myself the question, "Why me?" I find myself reigning in the future. I don't think years out anymore. As a matter of fact, I don't think too much about the future at all. I just think of what I can do now and plan accordingly. I think that some of the speed bumps that I worked through as a young man—divorce, father dying early, parents' bankruptcy when I was twelve. All had a tempering effect. I take pride in emotional strength and my relationship with God, but that does not mean that I am never down. Wednesday, I was down. I looked at my foot on the floor, and no matter what I did, I could not raise my foot or toes. Yes, I can raise my knee, and the foot follows; however, the foot is gone, never to return. My surgeon told the radiologist that he was probably taking the peroneal nerve. That pretty much is the whole enchilada as far as the lower leg and foot and toes are concerned. I was maintaining hope that the radiation would shrink the tumor and allow the surgeon to save the nerve. That just is not in the cards now. The good news is that I have a shiny new cane that my father-in-law loaned me. It's all ready to go, but I am trying not to use it too soon. Now "I want" the surgeon to be aggressive. I want the cancer out, never to return, but there are no guarantees in life.

I must share this with you. I have been bummed all day thinking about it. My wife, Cindy, got a call from one of her old friends at Wesleyan, where she used to work. One of the administrative assistant's husbands woke up yesterday with a sore left arm. He had breakfast with his wife and four-year-old son and then went off to give blood at the Red Cross. After that, he was off to work. They found him dead on the floor around 10:00 a.m., three hours after he reported his arm pain. *He was thirty-four years old!* If you feel a pain in your arm or chest that was not caused by yesterday's activity or an injury, go to the hospital and get it checked out. It also makes sense to "cowboy up" and make sure that you are square with God. We just don't know when death will claim us.

Okay, so the day went well as far as the radiation treatment is concerned. I swear that I can feel the radiation. It's a strange sensation that is not painful. It feels more like a progressive blush that spreads away from the tumor site and is very subtle.

All of the usual characters were there today, but at least one patient had finished up his radiation therapy and was missing. It's really funny: the patients speak so openly about their lives, families, diseases, etc., but ask a question about this person or that person from the staff, and good old "Hepa" steps in and "mums the word." We all laugh about it.

WRITTEN APRIL 17, 2010, 8:55 A.M.

Saturday morning update.

I forgot to mention to you that we had our appointment with the surgeon yesterday and the operation itself is being scheduled for about six to seven weeks from now. That should make it on just about ... *my birthday!* That is cruel. LOL

WRITTEN APRIL 17, 2010, 7:39 P.M.

And now we break for a public service announcement.

Cindy, my wife, is a director of MAPS (Middlesex Area Patient Services). MAPS works with patients suffering from multiple sclerosis (MS). MAPS raises money throughout the course of the year and spends 100 percent of it on services for people with MS. The directors are all unpaid volunteers, and MAPS tries to assist its patients with things like insurance deductibles, batteries for electric wheelchairs, and access ramps for their homes. MAPS also runs social events, such as an ice-cream and pizza social, an annual Christmas party, and a summer barbeque for the MS patients.

On May 1st, the Second Annual Motorcycle Poker Run will take place. If you know of anyone with a motorcycle who would like to have some fun for a good cause, please pass along the below website information. Everything they will need to know is on the site.

www.maps4ms.org

WRITTEN APRIL 19, 2010, 9:33 P.M.

Day twenty-six of twenty-eight (two days left!)

Time just seems to be whizzing by right now. I can't believe that I have been through five full weeks of radiation already and will finish up on Wednesday this week! There may be a short run of radiation after the surgery, if the doctors think that we need insurance. I still don't have to use the cane, so that's good. I was active today. That helped the lymphedema I have in that leg. Sometimes the swelling really hurts, and I have to lie down on the couch and put the leg up on the back to get the fluids to run back down toward my heart. The lymphedema is a side effect of my treatment for high blood pressure. If I am willing to stroke out, then I can reduce my leg swelling. No thanks. I saw both my mom and dad die of strokes, and their helplessness was frightening to me.

The actual date for surgery should be set by this Wednesday, but we expect it to be early June. My grandkids, Erica's children from Minneapolis, Nicolas and Lara, will be visiting in July. I hope I will be able to toddle around well enough to take them fishing at my favorite farm pond! Sunnys, bluegills, and smallmouth bass in great quantity, and they are delicious on the grill.

I decided what I am going to do for my five radiation therapists. First, I am writing each a personal note and enclosing a quantity of lottery tickets. In addition, I am writing a letter to Mr. Clarence Silva, the president of the hospital, praising each by name. I originally thought that I would enclose a copy of my letter in each of the notes, but I think that it should filter down from the top.

Cindy is making good progress on the jigsaw puzzle in the cancer center and has concluded that when she is done with the structural pieces for the windmill, she is going to leave the solid blue sky pieces for someone else.

I think I have made it clear over the years to most of my friends and relatives how wonderful my marriage with Cindy has been. She at once has been my best friend and lover, rock and femme fatale*. She has her own MS demons to contend with, and yet she has the strength and grace to support me a big sissy of a man who likes being Cindy's number one. Cindy and I sometimes are amazed at the terrible hurt the Women's Lib movement has perpetrated on the average woman. Somewhere along the way, the libbers have convinced women that supporting their men and birthing and raising their babies cannot be a fulfilling "career." We say, "Oh, contraire," but then how does one convince the young when they cannot understand until that age thing is handled and the gray hair of wisdom begin to sprout.

*Alluring and seductive woman whose charms ensnare her lover in bonds of irresistible desire.

PS: Cindy chided me tonight, saying that I might be getting onto my soapbox a little too much. I realize that I have a bully pulpit here, and my apologies go out to anyone I offend with my rambling. I hope that even with the pompous positions I sometimes take, you will understand that I am one man speaking with no fear of argument, as I have the microphone.

WRITTEN APRIL 20, 2010, 4:46 P.M.

Day twenty-seven of twenty-eight. (Last radiation day is tomorrow.)

The note cards with lottery tickets in them went over very well. All of the therapists were pleased, and I got a couple of hugs to boot. The radiation treatment went well after a slight adjustment based on yesterday's four X-rays. At least once per week during my treatment, they did a complete set of X-rays to be certain they were still aiming the gun in the correct direction. Today they moved the machine from a 95mm setting to a 94mm setting. That is a crazy small adjustment, considering my wedding band is five millimeters wide. So 1mm is about the thickness of a number-two pencil line.

Big news today is that my operation date has been set for May 25th. I will be missing the flyover of the Durham, CT, Memorial Day Parade, as well as my opportunity to march in it as an elected official, but Cindy has said that she will tell me all about it and bring pictures to the hospital when she comes to visit.

I was told in the beginning that I would be in hospital for about seven days and then would perhaps go to a rehab center to learn how to deal with the permanent damage to the leg. I will not be allowed to leave either place until I can climb fourteen stairs. That is the number of stairs between our garage and the living level of our house. I could be driven up on the front lawn, and then it would be four stairs. Cindy and I have been thinking of running a driveway right up the front lawn to our house entrance, but water runoff and other factors would need to be factored into a project like that.

So I need another pre-op physical from my primary care physician, blood work, suspension of Coumadin therapy, and visits to my cardiologist, surgeon, and radiologist for checkups before the hospital is willing to knock me out for several hours while someone "reconstructs my leg." I still do not like the name they have for the operation—"leg reconstruction." I think "leg alteration" sounds nicer or perhaps "leg fine-tuning." It will be interesting to see if they want yet another round of CAT scans. I did not like the last set. I will request sedation this time.

I guess I should tell you that my leg is still quite swollen around the tumor, although the radiologist does expect that it will shrink some prior to surgery. The radiation has burned the skin to a bright red and shiny state, and I use a special water-based cream on it as often as I think of it. Strangely, there is no pain on the tumor itself, but I cannot lay on that (my favorite side) in bed. The entire lower leg is quite tight and painful if any but the smallest movements are attempted. The most painful time for me is when I struggle to lift my toes. They shout back at me pretty loud.

Dr. G hasn't bought a boat yet, and I kind of hope he doesn't. He is not the kind of guy that can look philosophically at a boat. He still thinks that if you spend more money, it should be built better than a less expensive boat. I have found that to specifically not be the case. For example, a Sundancer thirty-four footer. (over $300,000) has an electric lift that raises the heavy batteries up for service, after first electrically opening a hatch cover. It also has a very badly engineered battery charger/maintainer. The result being that the single biggest problem Sundancer has is their batteries go dead a lot. As a result, the hatch doesn't open, and the batteries don't get raised for service. When contacted by owners, Sundancer thought that it might be a good idea for owners to upgrade their battery chargers to another brand, but Sundancer has made no changes to their offering.

WRITTEN APRIL 21, 2010, 9:33 P.M.

Day twenty-eight of twenty-eight. (My radiation is done, and my leg looks done to.)

I officially said good-bye to my cancer team at the George Bray Cancer Center in New Britain at the Hospital of Central Connecticut. I was happy to be done, but I met some truly outstanding people there. I was asked if I might consider returning to speak at one of their support groups. I am not sure that they would all understand where I get my composure. I bet they would all have kittens if I started talking about Jesus as the source of my peace.

I met with Lisa, the head nurse there, and she gave me the rundown on what I must do to promote healing, namely frequent applications of a water-based cream so that the skin does not dry out and crack. They don't want infection in there, and neither do I. No scrubbing, scratching, etc. Don't try to wash off the tattoos. Leg must not be exposed to the sun for one year, and during the second year, I must wear SPF 50 sunblock. I can go swimming but only after the surgeon has cleared me for it and only with cover-ups on.

My surgery is scheduled for May 25th, and all the doctors want me in to see them prior to that. I will be quite busy in May.

I will be slowing the journal down now that I do not have daily procedures. I expect to be in touch once per week or so.

Chapter 3

Pre-Op Patience

Written April 23, 2010, 8:32 p.m.

Okay, I lied. I won't be waiting a week between journal entries. Too much is happening around me and to me.

It's Friday night, and I am really excited to be going to New Jersey tomorrow for my grammar school fiftieth anniversary reunion. I attended a Catholic grammar school, Sacred Heart School, and have many great memories of my time there (1951–60). My dad owned a hardware store near the school, and he supplied most of the school's paint and hardware needs. My brother, Frank, was the school carpenter the whole time I was there.

I can remember it well when the nuns brought their large Virgin Mary statue to my dad to repair. He spent hours in the basement, mixing paint and touching up Mary's face. When he was done, it didn't look very realistic to me, but the nuns seemed to like it.

I have two older brothers: Frank, who is now seventy-eight years old and attended SHS from 1937 to 1946, and Joe, who is now seventy-two and attended SHS from 1943 until 1952. Between the store and my two brothers before me, the Sisters of Charity, who ran the school, really got to know my family well. My little sister, Annmarie, was born in 1956, and she attended SHS as well. If you do the math, you will find that my mother's first child was born in 1932, and her last was in 1956. That's quite a long and productive period. We all joke about it and say that she had four "only children" as there were six, eight, and ten years separating her pregnancies..

Tomorrow, I will be seeing friends I haven't seen since then, and I wonder how we will hit it off. In kindergarten, the class did a little skit on marriage, and Anita was my bride. We said all the vows and even kissed. Anita will be there with her husband, Frank. By the way, Anita is the same girl I danced with at the "Balloon Dance" we had in eighth grade. She sent me a picture of that dance, and it is in my Facebook pictures.

In a balloon dance, the boy and girl put their hands behind their backs and balance a balloon between the bridges of their noses. That is as close to girl contact as we got in 1960. Charlotte was my schoolmate throughout my SHS years as well. She returned to SHS as a teacher for several years. She is working on the

reunion committee. Thank you, Charlotte. I am looking forward to seeing you again.

Rich will be there. I remember playing together a couple of times, and I think his dad was in law enforcement—maybe a Newark policeman or detective. Rich and I went on to a Catholic high school together in Newark, but we had different friends based on the buses that we each took to get there. I took the 82 Bus and got dropped off at the "City Subway Station" on Bloomfield Avenue in Newark. From there, it was about a two-thirds-mile walk over the Second Avenue hill to our huge Essex Catholic High School building. Best time for my commute was about forty-five minutes. Rich lived right off of Bloomfield Avenue in Bloomfield, so he could take the 29 or the 60 to the same station I got off at and walk the hill. Back in the 1960s, the hill was nothing. Now I would die trying to walk over that thing.

I have rekindled a relationship with several grammar school friends as a result of this reunion and Facebook. Not bad for a non-computer generation. I don't see many seniors on Facebook.

I now understand the radiation thing. They blast you with radiation until they start to do real damage to good tissue, and then they hope that they killed the cancer. I did well with it, but the last ten days were uncomfortable as I had a hard time sleeping. And during the day, I experienced random cramps in the lower leg as well as some shooting pains that get your attention. I am glad that the pains are not debilitating and are short-lived, but they do surprise me from time to time and make it impossible to stay in one position for any length of time. The lymphedema I have in the leg also creates a problem for me if I don't keep the leg elevated about half the time.

Cindy says hello to you all, and I have nominated her for "Living Saint of the Year." We are quite a pair. Cindy's MS and my cancer coming together in one house makes for interesting times. By the way, she is doing very well and leads a very active life caring for the house and spending as much time as possible with Vicki's children. We are looking forward to Cole and Laura's visit this summer. We plan on spoiling them as much as possible in the four days they will be with us.

As I look toward May 25th, I realize that I didn't ask enough questions of the doctor, so I am writing them down to ask him at my next visit. I did realize that I would need a large comfortable car to come home from the hospital (or go to rehab) in, and Al W.'s Lincoln town car has been offered. I have no idea how I am going to get in and out of a car with only one leg working. Hope those rehab folks at the hospital are miracle workers.

WRITTEN APRIL 25, 2010, 4:51 P.M.

I am paying the price for going to the reunion, but it was worth it.

I got to be with friends I had not seen for fifty years. Can't say they haven't changed a lot, but very good to see them all again. The buffet was fabulous, and the auditorium and school were very nicely decorated for the occasion. We overnighted in a Ramada Inn in Wayne, NJ. It was just remodeled, and it was very nice for just $74.00. And that included a great breakfast. My overnight was tough. When I use this leg for any length of time, it yells back at me pretty good. We left the reunion early, like around 10:00, but I didn't get to sleep until about 4:00 a.m. because of cramps, spasms, and skin sensitivity. I couldn't even put a sheet on the irradiated area.

On the way home, we called Tyson and Rachel, who live in Danbury, and went to Icharo's Hibachi Steak House in Newtown. Very nice show, good food, and a fun atmosphere with two special people.

Cindy and I finally got home around 4:00 p.m., and my leg is up now. I should have brought the OxyContin with me for last night, but I forgot all my meds at home.

WRITTEN APRIL 30, 2010, 12:40 A.M.

Sleep has been difficult this week. About half the time, it is as late as 4:00 a.m. before I get off to sleep. If I take a Percocet, it is earlier, so I am taking Percocet now. The radiation did a number on my leg, and it is badly swollen by midday unless I am really careful and keep it elevated. I have a man-cave that has a large sofa. It is large enough for me to lie down full length, and I can drape my leg over the back of the sofa to elevate it. That is the way I try to sleep. We are still using a special water-based cream, but the skin still is hypersensitive. At times—not all the time but at times—I cannot even put a sheet on the surface of the leg without real discomfort. The nurse at the cancer center mentioned that this might happen and suggested a soft man-made fabric. I bought two sets of sleeper pants made of that stuff, and they work well. I can cream up, slide into the pants, and feel relatively good. I have to ration my walking and sitting upright as the water runs right down into my feet again in no time. I take water pills twice a day, and that seems to help. I swear there are times when I just wish the leg was gone and I could get on with a peg leg. I no longer have a great attachment to this leg.

Many other aspects of life are great. At church, the care teams that I am involved with are making progress, and we have our second orientation meeting after church this Sunday. I am very proud of my step-daughter, Victoria, as she is openly affected, as I was, with the pleasure that we can bring to nursing home residents that don't see many visitors. We kind of just ask ourselves WWJD (What would Jesus do?) and do it. When you understand the ropes, it's easy to sit down and chat with many of these residents, and they all have great stories and commonsense wisdom that they have earned over their lifetimes. They are a hidden and silent natural resource that is available to any who want it. Visit a nursing home and see for yourself. You will get more from it than you give.

I have been shooting a couple of times at my sportsman's club in the past couple of weeks and enjoyed it a lot. I have a wonderful collection of weapons and was first exposed to the bullet-reloading process over fifty years ago by my older brother, Frank. He gave me his old red "Lyman All American" press, and I have added three more turret presses to further automate the process. I am just one of many hundreds of thousands of sportsman who enjoy shooting sports and the occasional harvesting of game. I also enjoy fishing. I have a farmer's pond waiting for a worm and a two-pound test line on an ultra light rod I made myself at age eighteen. That rod will go to a grandchild who takes on the sport. I run up from that ultra-light to five foot boat poles with 110-pound test line just in case I hit something big in saltwater. I am fortunate to have been able to land a 744-pound giant blue fin tuna back in the early 90s, and my agreement with God at the time was that I never had to catch another fish in my lifetime, if He would only let me land that thing. It is more than a fish story, as I have most of the event on a VHS tape that I dust off and watch from time to time. I am a very blessed guy, and God's gifts to me go beyond my understanding. I pray that you all could know Him as I attempt to. It has been a life-changing awakening for me.

By now you are probably wondering if the Percocet has taken me over the edge, and maybe tonight, it has a bit. I have really enjoyed writing all of the journal entries, and I hope that some of what I am writing will mean something to my grandchildren after I am gone—and I don't plan for that to happen anytime soon, so please don't think I am being morbid. This is my second time around with cancer. The first time was three years ago, and I had a lymphoma removed from my back. It was a fast treatment plan with no radiation or chemo, just the surgery, and I was back on my motorcycle on a trip to Niagara Falls about three weeks after the surgery. That time around, it got my attention for a while, but it was not a real scare at the time. Perhaps I was a Polly Anna then. This time around, my hands are full, and I have had lots of time to think. Your point of view takes a big change when your concerns are real. You guys have been great, and no one has told me that I am wacky or just plain nuts. I know that I am long-winded sometimes, but I seem to be able to say what is really important to me in these journal entries. If I have offended anyone's sensibilities, I hope you will dismiss my ramblings as those of a threatened species speaking out while the speaking is good. I really do have so many things that I want you to know about me. Perhaps the most important thing that I have to say to you tonight (after my references to God) is that I really am very sure that I am not a one-act play with you playing bit parts in my life. Each of you, without exception, has impacted me in ways that you will probably never know. You have made a difference in my life, and for that, I thank you. Many of you have shown me your soft underbelly, and I pray that I did not abuse that privilege. I guess in many ways, I am trying to do the same in the hopes that I may be more than a passing character in your lives. I can say this to you: It is a very gratifying feeling to know that you are surrounded by truly good friends. You who are reading this today mean more to me than you will ever know. Lights are going out here at 2:00 a.m. Thank you, Bristol-Meyers.

WRITTEN MAY 3, 2010, 9:42 P.M.

I am having a hard time answering my friends now when they ask how I feel, how I'm doing, if the leg is feeling better, etc.

Here is why.

This is all new to me. I flat out do not know what to expect during this "second phase" of my treatment. I know that I am supposed to be "healing" right now … but not from the cancer. I am healing from the damage they did to me with the radiation. I am healing so that they can operate on May 25th. I will be in hospital for five to seven days and then staying in rehab to learn to walk again. I hope they killed the cancer with the radiation, but the tumor is still the same size it was when I started treatment, so I don't really know.

So let's summarize:

Phase one: Radiation is over.

Phase two: "Post-radiation" started with poor sleep, cramps, shooting pains, and numbing sensations. They all got worse for about a week after the radiation ended. On a scale of one to ten, the worst pains were fours; however, their number grated on me, and I have felt sorry for myself a couple of times.

Now I hope I am entering the middle part of phase two. The leg seems uncomfortably dull. The top of the foot is in "pins and needles," and the bottom sometimes feels numb ... but less than a week ago. I am beginning to wonder if the radiation didn't do some temporary nerve damage and if I might get some healing of the nerve before surgery. The radiologist had said that he hoped to minimize damage to the peroneal nerve, but apparently, there was some. I still can't lift my toes, but I can tilt my foot back a little. The bright red burn from the radiation is turning to a deep brown tan, and small areas (in spite of constant lotion) have peeled, revealing red skin underneath. I have little pep and energy, and I must rest in between physical effort lasting more than several minutes. If my leg is vertical, it fills up with water unless I am walking, and that feels unsteady. I am resisting the cane until I can find one with a sword or gun in it.

I am hoping that the tumor begins to shrink, that my lymph edema gets better, and that I can maintain a more comfortable sleeping position. Last night was the first night I was able to sleep on my left side.

To give you an idea of the size of the tumor, measuring my right "good leg" around is seventeen inches. Measuring the bad left leg at the calf muscle is nineteen inches.

I have received several comments that the CaringBridge site is a very good way to communicate, so if you have any questions that you think I can answer, please ask them in the guestbook, and I will take a whack at them as time is available.

Good night, and don't forget your prayers.

In Your hands,
Bob

WRITTEN MAY 5, 2010, 8:54 P.M.

Today was the best day that I have had since about midway through the radiation treatment. I have only a slight limp, and the burn on the leg is healing nicely. Cindy rubs lotion into it a couple of times a day. I remember a couple of weeks ago that the lotion hurt. Now it is a pleasant sensation as long as she doesn't push too hard. The shooting pains have stopped, and I almost had myself believing that I could feel more in the foot; however, that is not true.

It is strange to be excited about "getting better" while at the same time I know that I have a date with the knife on May 25th.

I was really surprised that I was able to work most of yesterday at the polling place without swelling too badly. Thanks, Cari, for the comment on the lymph edema and physical therapy. I will discuss that with the doctors next week.

WRITTEN MAY 9, 2010, 10:40 P.M.

It is Sunday night, and I have not added anything to the journal since Wednesday. Things are pretty much the same. My leg continues to "heal." The red is gone, and I feel that I can do a little more with it each day. Today, I actually did a couple of chores outside and managed okay until I sat down. It is strange. It seems that I do well while I am active, but then all Hades breaks lose when I sit or lay down. I need to be careful when I rest. I cannot stretch the leg out straight when I lie down as I get almost immediate pain right behind the knee, almost as if I was stretching a tendon or something. I am down to my last Percocet. I took one around 7:30 tonight just to get some relief. Enough about the pain. The worst thing going on right now is a mind game. I am plumb out of patience and can't wait for this operation. I have been dealing with this thing since late January or so, and it is May without a final determination of anything. My leg measures 18.75 inches around, so it has gone down a quarter inch, but with the edema and all, I can't tell if it is a real reduction or not. I tried out the cane while I was shopping at Cabela's yesterday and hate it.

Thomas the Tank Engine was in Essex this weekend. I miss having "something" to do with that event. The kids are so excited to see Thomas that it is infectious. If you have grandkids or children, Thomas will be there again next weekend. You will be building special memories that last forever. Oh, how I remember when my parents used to take me to New Jersey's "Gingerbread Castle." I can never forget it, and neither will these kids forget Thomas. Full-sized steam locomotives are almost extinct. The old equipment is getting older, and the knowledge base of how to repair these things is doing the same. You should not wait any longer to introduce your kids to the iron horses that connected sea to shining sea.

I have received lots of nice guestbook entries from family and friends. It is nice to hear from each of you. I have two doctor's appointments this week and will let you know what is happening after Wednesday. Thanks for reading.

Written May 11, 2010, 10:48 p.m.

This is pre-op checkup week and *thirteen days until surgery.*

On Monday, I had my pre-op physical with my primary care physician. Heart EKG and blood pressure all were good. A CBC lab test was done as well. I have been going to Dr. S since 1974. His was a new practice in the Grove Hill Clinic in New Britain at that time. We have been friends ever since, and we have visited each other's homes, gone boating, etc. Dr. S is a very good doctor. It may sound melodramatic, but Dr. S found my first cancer during an annual physical and may have saved my life. Another time, he saved me from unnecessary surgery by convincing the hospital to allow me several more days and two transfusions before they removed my colon. My internal bleeding spontaneously stopped on its own. I get a chill just thinking about that one, but that is why I drive twenty-five miles to my doctor.

On Tuesday (today), we met with our surgeon, Dr. F, for the last exam prior to surgery. He described what he was going to do in greater detail while he made no assurances, as he has to have the freedom to do what is needed. I had to "sign off" that I understood what he was being authorized to do. The procedure is called "radical lower-leg reconstruction," not a terribly comforting description. I guess the good news is that he will not be taking complete muscles but about half of the calf muscle and half of another muscle. In addition, the peroneal nerve and most likely the fibula bone (which he assures me I don't need) also look like toast. The cancer is currently encased in "good flesh," and he will remove it while it remains completely encased in a "safe margin" of tissue. He does not want to see the cancer itself until it is outside the body. He will not be creating an incision and then spreading the skin open to work. He will be taking the full surface of the leg down to the depth of the safe margin. The result will be a very large hole about six or seven inches long by two and a half inches wide down to the bone. It will be in the shape of a football. In order to close this hole he will be taking skin grafts from my thigh. The skin graft stuff was new information and a bit unnerving. Everything I find on the web about skin grafts mentions pain—oh, and have I mentioned I am a baby when it comes to pain? I had the doctor explain in detail how the whole process works. He was a hoot describing all of the neat tools he got to use. I have to admit that it is avant-garde stuff ... but unnerving at the same time. I'll let you know whether you should queue up for this procedure just yet! LOL.

The doctor thinks five days in the hospital and then rehab. I will be six weeks on crutches and obviously on my back most of the time. I am having a wrought iron railing installed on the front porch as well as railings on both sides of the interior stairwell. The air-conditioning people were here today, and they are working on installing AC in the "man-cave," which until now was not insulated in the cathedral ceiling because I loved the sound of rain on the roof. The room has a gas fireplace in it, but I had hot water baseboard heat put in it right after the insulation went in, and now the AC will finish the job ... just in time for our town-wide reevaluation. Durham does have a good deal for seniors. Next year, when I hit sixty-five years old, my taxes will be frozen and will not go up ever again. That is just one of the reasons we really want to stay in this town in retirement.

On Wednesday (tomorrow), I have an appointment at the hospital for the hospital's own pre-op workup. They will do blood-typing, evaluate my current meds, and tell me which ones to take on the morning I check into the hospital. They also ask a million questions, like the one where they ask who your pastor is and the church's phone number. Hello, are you hinting at something here? After that screening, I have my final nuclear CAT scan. The surgeon wants a final picture of the mass of capillaries that are all connected to the cancer. They will inject me with a sugar solution that has been irradiated. Because cancer loves sugar, the irradiated sugar will clearly outline the cancer in the CAT scan.

Oh, and one more thing, I got the bill for the radiation—only $42,827.43

WRITTEN MAY 14, 2010, 11:12 P.M.

It's kind of easy to become self-occupied when you get caught up in a serious illness and everyone around you is so supportive. I have had a reality check this week. Cindy's cousin, John, from her family living up on the cape is in the hospital with what may be an advanced stage of lung cancer. Everything is happening so quickly that we don't even have a clear diagnosis yet, but it is very serious.

I ask that you include John on your prayer lists, praying that he not only is healed from his illness but also that he may find God and peace in the process.

WRITTEN MAY 16, 2010, 7:33 P.M.

Cindy and I had a wonderfully relaxing Friday and Saturday at home. The umbrella on the deck cut down the direct sunlight and made for a cozy little place to sit and talk. We cooked and ate out there too. It has been a long time since we did that, and we want to do it more often.

Sunday was a little different. I slept until 9:15 a.m., which is very unusual for me; however, I have had trouble sleeping the last week or so, and I took a pain med around 5:00 a.m. on one of my trips to the bathroom. I dropped back into a deep sleep, and Cindy moving around and showering never disturbed me. The rest of the day was spent trying to manage the nervousness I am starting to feel as we get closer to May 25th. The whole day came to a crashing end when we got the call that our cousin Johnny up on Cape Cod had died earlier this morning. His daughter, who graduated yesterday, did get to see and talk to him, but he was pretty well out of it. At least they saw each other.

John had gone to a doctor, concerned over a pain in his leg, which prevented him from working. The doctor heard his coughing and suggested a chest X-ray. That was two weeks ago. We finally have the diagnosis from the biopsy, a huge lung cancer that spread to his brain, resulting in the strokes. He passed away peacefully at 9:15 a.m. this morning. I don't know if he knew the Lord, but I pray that God's love and mercy will show itself. Please pray for John's mom, Margaret, and his siblings, Anne, Lynn, Mark, and Stephen.

WRITTEN MAY 22, 2010, 12:39 A.M.

This is the last weekend before my date with the surgeon on Tuesday. I am looking forward to finally taking some decisive action against this cancer.

My radiologist was the last doctor I saw this week, and he was disappointed that the cancer swelling has not reduced as a result of the radiation. My leg is still nineteen inches around as it has been for months now. He was fast to state that the fact the swelling hadn't gone down had nothing to do with the efficacy of the radiation treatment.

As for me, I am ready to get something done finally.

I met with the surgeon earlier in the week, and I know that I mentioned that he was now planning for skin grafts to cover up the "open pit mine" that he is going to carve in my leg. I have been real good up until now, but I must admit to having the jitters for the past several days. The long time line between diagnosis, radiation treatment, healing from the radiation, and now four months later finally "excavating" was the worst part of this thing.

Now I am more bothered by the idea of catheters, crutches, bedpans, and boredom than anything. Heck, I have already read every Louis L'Amour book that I could get my hands on ... like about eighty of his 140 books. What else can I start to read? Are there any classics beyond Louis?

My wife, Cindy, has been a great nurse through this whole thing, and my thanks go out to you for staying up on the details through this website. The phones have been quiet. I will be showing Cindy how to log in as me, and she will pass along a short informational "journal" after Tuesday's operation as I plan to be in la-la land for as long as they can keep me there. See you on the other side!

WRITTEN MAY 23, 2010, 2:12 P.M.

If you have read my last journal entry, I am sure you thought that you wouldn't hear from me until Cindy wrote with the operation results. I kind of thought that as well. So why am I writing again? For two reasons—

First, at church today, a very wonderful thing happened. Our pastor spoke about my long relationship with the church and said that we are a "praying" church. He then invited everyone to extend their hands toward me and pray with him for my surgery and recovery. It was the equivalent of early Christians placing their hands upon the person for whom they prayed. At the same time, it was very public and very personal for me. It was our common acknowledgment that God's grace and our trust in Him is what was needed in the situation. Very moving.

I am very thankful for the "calm which passeth all understanding" that came over me from the beginning. I don't want anyone to say, "Boy, Bob, seems to have it all together," or "Look how great he is doing." Rather please acknowledge with me the supernatural gift of grace that God has given me. He is carrying me on His back through these rough waters, and He has been consistently by my side through all the treatments so far. He is even with me when I lose sight of Him, when I fear or begin to feel sorry for myself. All I have to do is remember His importance to me, and He is there in crystal clarity. All glory be given to You, oh, Lord.

Secondly, I again want to thank each of you who have taken the time to read my journals. I am sure they got very old. I don't know how I would have been able to communicate with all of my friends without wanting to shoot myself because of the necessary repetition. My phone has been reasonably quiet, something that I could not expect without "CaringBridge." After the surgery, we expect a long convalescence, and yes, I will continue to bore you with journal entries. But I want you all to know that we look forward to your visiting as well. I plan to have a slide presentation of the operation and ... kidding! LOL

WRITTEN MAY 25, 2010, 6:49 A.M.

No operation today!

I do not know where to begin. We were getting ready to leave for the hospital when the phone rang at 6:15 this morning, and it was my surgeon on the phone. He apologized profusely for calling at the eleventh hour, but he admitted that he was troubled yesterday and lost sleep last night as he prepared himself for my procedure. I have already told you that the tumor has not shrunk after the radiation treatment. He was much more pessimistic about whether the radiation worked than the radiologist was. The shrinkage was meant to be a prime indicator that the surgeon's decisions about what to remove from my leg were valid assumptions. As the surgeon reviewed his notes, CAT scans, PET scans, etc., he realized that without the shrinkage, his plan was very risky for me. His good attempt to save some movement and use could basically kill me. Unfortunately, we had to get into the survival numbers, and here they are. Assuming I had the operation as planned and all worked out, my survival for five years is 50 percent. If he made a mistake and was too optimistic and the tumor returned, my survival rate drops to 10 to 15 percent. This cancer is a bad one that does not respond well to chemo or surgery if it reaches the chest cavity. The more cautious approach, which he now believes we must take, is to get a second opinion from a doctor in Hartford who is the only orthopedic oncologist in the area. That second opinion could happen as early as today, and an operation scheduled "very soon." The second opinion is needed because the recommendation now is that we do this operation as planned but take the tumor to the lab for immediate testing, and if not totally dead, they will return to the operating table and remove my leg above the knee. We continue to bear up okay, but I will not "guild the lily." Sometimes life is not a box of chocolates. This is not fun right now.

I will be back to you after the second opinion.

Written May 25, 2010, 5:06 p.m.

Today was terrible!

I cannot begin to explain to you how I feel right now. It is so confusing! Today's surgery was cancelled, and Cindy and I have an appointment to see a well-known orthopedic oncologist at St. Francis Hospital on Thursday at 8:00 a.m. in Hartford in order to seek a second opinion on the specific operation that I need. I am told that this doctor in Hartford (in discussion with my doctor in New Britain) is sympathetic toward amputation but "wants to see all of the films." That is where Cindy and I come in.

Today was spent driving around to our doctor's office and to the hospital to obtain the films and reports in question. While we were on the move, we decided to eat in the hospital cafeteria as it has great offerings at reasonable prices and it is one floor up from the radiology department, where our films were. What happened there comes right out of the *Twilight Zone*.

As I was walking around and making my selections, I saw my radiologist. When he saw me, he did a double take as he knew that I was scheduled for surgery. He asked me what was going on, and when I told him, he was surprised. He immediately took the position that I did not need an amputation and that before I did allow one, he wanted me to wait for an appointment at Sloan Kettering Institute in NYC. A million thoughts rushed into my mind about who should make my decisions for treatment. I was sure that the person making them should not be me! Am I right? It seems that I am in the middle of a disagreement between three doctors on what to do. The radiologist prefaced his statements by saying that he "was not a surgeon, but if it were my leg being amputated, Sloan Kettering would be doing the job." My radiologist is an extremely alpha male with a fantastic reputation, and I was told by my surgeon's nurse that they received a call from him within minutes of my encountering him in the cafeteria. I agreed with my radiologist to call him after my appointment for the second opinion in Hartford on Thursday.

I am in a dust cloud of indecision right now, when all I really want is clarity and decisive treatment of this leg. Cindy is now scared that the cancer is growing in my body while the doctors decide whose sandbox to play in. Another opinion is that I am extremely fortunate that I have doctors willing to openly disagree and who all want what is best for me.

WRITTEN MAY 25, 2010, 8:14P.M.

If I didn't have CaringBridge and the sense that I have a lot of fine people like you pulling for me, I would be off somewhere in a corner, sucking my thumb and crying. My prayer for you is that you never have to use CaringBridge but that if you do, you will use it as I have to stay in touch with your friends and prayer partners. My faith and CaringBridge is the only comfort I now have. I ask you to pray especially for Cindy as she is very scared right now. Thank you.

WRITTEN MAY 26, 2010, 6:08 P.M.

Indecision: 0

Home Team: 1

No summary here. If you want to understand this one, please reread the last three journal entries.

Our appointment in Hartford is for 8:00 a.m. tomorrow, but Cindy and I decided to drive up to find the doctor's office and to drop off the CDs containing the CT, PET, and MRI scans. I was still pretty much a train wreck looking for a place to happen; however, the drive was okay, and we enjoyed side roads through West Hartford and Farmington on the way to lunch.

Cindy has poison ivy, so we had to call our primary physician for her steroid script, and because we ate at our favorite Chinese place in New Britain, we just decided to stop by the doctor's office to pick up my painkiller script as well. My primary physician is the guy I was bragging about who has treated me for thirty-five years and saved my life at least once. I hadn't called him when the operation had been cancelled as I wasn't sure I wanted to add another doctor's point of view into the discussion. I was really confused and mistaken, as I should have called Earl immediately. He was as upset over how everything came down as a professional will show and basically told me, "You are not going back to Dr. F. He is done with you." He went on to tell me that he and I would consult after each stage of the second-opinion process and decide whether I should go down to Memorial Sloan-Kettering Cancer Center (MSKCC) as Dr. G (my radiologist) insisted.

I could have cried when he took over the decision-making on this aspect of my treatment. The tension just flowed out of me, and I felt better than I have felt in a long time. My recommendation to you is to build a good rapport with your own professional care provider, whether it is an MD or a specialist. There may come a time, as it did with me, that you need a proactive, trusted friend to assist you with handling the super big decisions. It's funny. Now at least if I do lose my leg over this deal, I will at least know I had the very best advice.

WRITTEN MAY 27, 2010, 3:04 P.M.

Indecision: 0

Home Team: 2

Cindy and I left for the new hospital (St. Francis in Hartford) this morning at 6:30 for an 8:00 a.m. appointment. I am glad we did as the doctor was already there when we arrived at 7:30. He was able to start viewing our video MRI, CAT, and PET scan files even before we filled out the five pages of medical history that they need to have in order to register a new patient. Somewhere along the way, they figured out how to bill the insurance company as well.

We were ushered into first a waiting room and then within minutes into an examination room, and Dr. S was not far behind. The next hour and a half was spent with the doctor and his physician's assistant discussing the case. This doctor clearly knows about histeosarcomas and added great clarity to what we already knew. He has wonderful credentials: academic director of orthopedic surgery, director of musculoskeletal oncology, assistant professor at UConn Health Center for oncology, total joints, and trauma. Best of all, he describes his work as extremely close to the approaches used at Dana Farber and Sloan Kettering. He uses less chemotherapy but does use it.

Dr. S discussed just about every aspect of the case and then played my files for us on his computer. He walked Cindy and I through my current treatment, and what happened to the tumor while I was being treated. It was obvious that the tumor continued to grow until halfway through the radiation and then stopped. Toward the end of its growth, it squeezed up against the fibula and crushed the peroneal nerve, the thing that I have been trying to save. It also has thinned out the skin covering the tumor to the point where he may have to graft skin not only for coverage but for strength. He related about one patient who only came to him after the tumor had ruptured through the skin and began draining outside the body. Mine was not anywhere near that stage, but it is considered a high-risk tumor because of its large size (6 by 14.6cm) and its fast growth. He is anxious to operate, and we have set June 11th as the day.

The operation will take about seven to eight hours and involve his doing what is called a "radical leg reconstruction." At this point, it is not a guarantee that the leg gets saved. I had to sign and permit him to amputate right over the knee joint if, when he gets in there, he finds that the cancer has crossed boundaries that are considered safe. Just like in the movies, I will not know if I have a leg until the anesthesia wears off and I wake up in the hospital room. Because of the blood loss and transfusions, I may be in intensive care for a couple of days afterward. He thinks the hospital stay will be between four to eight days, depending on how everything goes.

Histeosarcoma metastasizes through the bloodstream, usually to the lungs, and the follow-up after surgery is not to watch the leg but to have CAT scans of the lungs every three months. The mortality rates did not change from my previous journal entries.

Cindy and I already like St. Francis (I guess any port in a storm) and are somewhat relieved that we do not have to go to NYC in order to get informed, quality care for this rare cancer.

More blood was taken today, another MRI tomorrow, and another physical next week and then some waiting until the 11th. I will be doing some shooting on Saturday with my friend Scott and generally looking to reduce the strain. My BP in the doctor's office was 180/110.

Cindy and I now know we have done what we humanly can do to fight this disease. The rest is up to God, and I place my total trust in Him who is my savior. If the cancer isn't stopped and He ultimately takes me, please know that I have just been called home. I will be happy to be there, reunited with friends and family, awaiting your arrival. Of course, that is … if you arrive. You have been invited. Have you accepted?

Written May 28, 2010, 9:19 p.m.

It's 8:20 p.m., and I'm finally home. Cindy and I worked like a tag team on the garage today. I had a chair sitting there, and I would work for five minutes and sit down for ten. Things got done, but not very quickly. LOL

At 2:30 p.m., we headed out for the Hospital of Central Connecticut to the pathology lab to pick up the glass slides that they made up of my cancer biopsy. Our new doctor, Dr. S, doesn't like to read reports. He likes to diagnose based on his own interpretation of data. The actual slides moving from the old to the new hospital is an example.

At 4:15 p.m., I reported as ordered to St. Francis Hospital's MRI machine. After I filled out four more sheets of paperwork, they had me in the MRI machine from 4:45 until 6:30 p.m. I was in pain, and had to go to the bathroom and was frazzled with the Spanish singing that I had to listen to on their machine's headphones. I asked for classical music. The first CD was all Wagner—just great ... not, and the second CD was the Spanish singing. It was a laughable situation, and I was totally strapped down, so I could not move from the waist down. I don't want to sound like I'm complaining, but it's just that it was over the top. I had to laugh in spite of the pain. Hey, maybe that's the master plan. At least my claustrophobia didn't kick in as I was only in the machine up to about mid-stomach.

When I was done, I couldn't move my left leg, and they had to help me off the table and get me to my feet. They sent someone to walk with me a ways as I was unsteady on the left leg. The foot is dropping more, and I fell twice today, catching myself in a doorway once and on a hospital handrail the second time. My loafers with rubber soles for boating are real grippers on polished surfaces. If my foot drops at all, the shoe comes to a skidding stop before it passes under my center of gravity, and down I go. I have to think through each step to lift that leg.

I haven't been using a cane, so I did not have anything to help me out. It was pretty embarrassing when I stumbled right in front of the hospital's information desk. They wanted to call transportation for an electric cart to take me to MRI. Had I known at the time that MRI was about a two-hundred-yard walk, I would have taken them up on it.

We missed Bennett's science fair at his school because I was so long in the MRI machine. Bennett did extremely well, earning a perfect score on all seven criteria for the project. We have a one-minute video of him explaining the project, and I hope Vicki posts it to her Facebook page.

When we got home, I sanded down an old, natural color cane I have and stained it dark walnut. A coat of poly tomorrow, a new rubber bumper, and *voila*, all set.

Next medical matter to handle is my third pre-op physical next Wednesday. Pray that three is a lucky number for me.

Hey, for those of you that remember my cousin John from Cape Cod, who died very suddenly last week, his memorial service was Thursday, and here is what they did. The family placed lilies in his fishing boots, and they had his clam rakes and gear nicely laid out with flowers. His ashes were sealed in his tackle box, and everything was buried with him and covered over, not with dirt but with crushed clam shells. I guess that is considered a proper Cape Cod send-off.

WRITTEN MAY 30, 2010, 2:52 P.M.

I am pleased to tell you that absolutely nothing has happened in the past two days, and Cindy and I are enjoying this Memorial Day weekend.

Tomorrow, we hope to attend the world-renowned Durham Memorial Day Parade, and we plan to get there by lawn tractor and trailer.

WRITTEN JUNE 2, 2010, 12:03 P.M.

This morning, I had my third pre-op physical. This was hopefully my last physical before the operation on June 11, 2010.

As you may remember, my first "emergency operation" was cancelled when the pre-op CAT scan came back suggesting that the cancer had spread to my lungs. I was sent into a long radiation treatment plan and then a longer healing process in order to get ready for the second surgery.

On the morning of the second surgery, my doctor called and essentially "bailed," saying he was no longer sure that he could perform the surgery without placing my life in danger. He referred me to the "grand Poobaa" of cancer surgeons at St. Francis Hospital in Hartford. My new doctor is more versed in this type of operation, and he is proceeding with it. I am told that the operation will be seven to eight hours long, with my surgeon turning it over to a plastic surgeon to "close." I trust that I will be in la-la land and my wife on pins and needles the whole time. There is risk that I will lose the leg just above the knee, if, when the doctor opens it up, he doesn't like what he finds.

The waiting around has been a tempering process for Cindy and me. We turn often to God for comfort, and it is freely gifted.

I have learned a lot during the past five months. Slowing down as I have gives way more time to experience life in Technicolor. Family and friends become very important. Old favorite moments are absolutely huge now! I had a fiftieth grammar school reunion to attend, so I got to go back to my hometown and look once again at the streets and houses of childhood. Some of what I have learned from all this was enjoyable and some heartbreaking. Memories from my youth that had grown disproportionately over the years came crashing down by just a small touch of reality, while several of my friendships have blossomed in the sunlight and rain of attention. Life for me is forever changed by this illness, my relationships strengthened, and my point of view shifted. All in all, it has been an E ticket ride this year.

Now again is the wait, this time for June 11th. I have become good at it. As a matter of fact, I am proud of the way I wait. I may wait better than anyone I know. I envision lesser men secreting themselves away or screaming into the dark, wanting to know what is happening. Not me, I take my blanky and my bottle and sit down in the corner, suck my thumb, and wait.

WRITTEN JUNE 4, 2010, 7:05 P.M.

I am so deeply moved by the outpouring of feelings that I have received on the phone, in person, and on this website. People have been saying wonderful things, beautiful prayers, and just acting like good friends during this entire journey. Today, I had a surprise visit from a friend I have not seen in years. I thought he was visiting from East Haddam after shopping in Middletown only to find out he had moved to Farmington about three years ago and he drove down from there.

Now things have finally slowed down, and Cindy and I can think again. I look over my shoulder to see where I have been, and all I see are my friends. I don't see the problems we have handled. You have carried me on your collective back for over four and a half months! You will never know how humble that makes me feel. All I can say is thank you.

I want to shout out to Steve in South Carolina, Paul, my oldest friend in California and Hawaii who sends weekly cards (but I don't think reads CaringBridge), Pam, who is one of my prayer warriors (and a great cook to boot), a couple of great Bobs who I worked for, Bruce at the RR, and young Michelle, who has a heart of gold dedicated to Jesus, Carlee, Shane, our almost family members Deb, Joan, Sandi, Pat, Marge, Big Mike, Kim, Mackenzie and so many others who have written, and a huge group, including my immediate family like Erica, Beth, Adam, and Vicki, who read faithfully of our journey and communicate in person and by phone. I have not counted but well over a hundred people stay involved. I honestly did not know the strength that could be gleaned from such contact, but I want you to know that I would be a nutcase if I tried to do this alone. I believe that good will come out of this ordeal through your prayers and encouragement and the power of Jesus Christ working with us.

Just thought that I needed to tell you this before I leave to get a dozen worms for me to take my grandson Bennett fishing tomorrow morning. Wish us luck!

PS: Thank you, Frank and Gerda, for the fabulous German meal and your overnight visit. It's nice to get some attention from a big brother.

WRITTEN JUNE 7, 2010, 4:50 P.M.

Inasmuch as I am sixty-four years old and inasmuch as I have fished my whole life, I do know that four- to six-year-olds need action, if you ever want to get them to fish as a hobby. About two years ago, I began looking for a place to fish that was very close to

my house and very full of fish. I found just the thing on a friend's farm, their farm pond. When you walk around the three-quarter-acre pond, you see fish looking right back at you. The bigger ones are smallmouth bass in the 1.5- to 2.0-pound size, while the smaller ones are what I call pumpkin seeds or bluegills in the eight- to ten-inch range. My friend told me that five-pound bass have been taken.

A worm on a hook with a bobber (best way for kids) yields a sunfish just about every cast. The biggest problem with them is getting them off the hook without killing them. They inhale that worm. The bass seem to respond best to a small trout spinner with a treble hook. Their mouths are plenty big to get the lure unsnarled without killing the fish. We fished for about an hour in the sun, and we caught a total of eight to ten fish. And about three of them were bass. I posted a couple of pictures, so check them out!

Chapter 4

THIRD TIME'S A CHARM!

WRITTEN JUNE 10, 2010, 3:46 P.M.

It looks as if the "third time is a charm." My surgery should go as scheduled for tomorrow.

Our alarm is set for an early start at 4:00 a.m. Friday morning. We have been asked to arrive at the hospital by 5:30 a.m. so that they may prep me for a 7:15 surgery. They tell me that the surgery could go eight hours long. (That is a little unnerving). A pre-op nurse called to work out what meds I should and should not take. Heck, I even know where to park.

The last few days have been trying. It was a struggle to stay in control of not so much the emotion as much as what I call the "worry factor." The surgery can go two ways: Either Dr. S accepts what he finds when he opens and he does a leg resection, or he rejects it and does an amputation. If he amputates, I have the best percentage for full recovery, 65 percent. If he saves the leg, there is more risk, but I will have a leg. The nerves will all be gone either way, so the leg would be semi-functional. At sixty-four years old, I have to factor in life expectancy either way—all very confusing. Perhaps the most maddening thing is that I am unable to discuss the options further with the doctor as I absolutely do not want to sway his judgment one way or the other. I am paying the best guy around to work on me, and the last thing I want is for him to feel any pressure relative to my preferences. There is a certain amount of melodrama here, as I will find out if I have a leg when I wake up. Many of you will know before me, because Cindy will be on the phone once she gets word of the operations completion. Cindy may mention something on my Facebook page, but more informative will be here on CaringBridge, too.

So finally, I ask one more time for your prayers for Dr. S so that he may skillfully practice his trade and that 100 percent of the cancer is removed. Whether I have my own leg or a bionic one is not what I ask you to pray about.

Final pre-op thought: This battle with cancer has been an incredible learning experience for me. It has taught me that we really do not have control over major parts of our lives. Sicknesses and ultimately dying are not for us to decide. There is either a coincidence that controls things (evolution) or an intelligent design (creationism and God) that does. For a major part of my life, I have camped firmly on the side of God and intelligent design. I had a conversation with Jesus last night, and lying there in bed, I could sense His closeness to me. He brought me contentment, comfort, and a better sleep than I have had in weeks. He knows that I am an imperfect creature, a repetitive sinner, but He also knows that I believe that He is the Son of God, who came to this earth to show us the way to salvation. I have placed all of this in His hands, and I am comfortable with whatever happens. I look forward to the lessons He will teach me and others through this journal and its guestbook entries.

This blog has had over three thousand visits since we started. I thank you for your patience and support. It is an incredibly nice thing to be able to feel the support of the friends that went through the "bumper car" ride called life with me. Your encouragements have been great! I wish each of you the best and hope that you have found this blog to have some temporal or spiritual value to you. I especially appreciate the patience of some of you who are unchurched. It must have been difficult for you to put up with my ravings. On the other hand, perhaps this journey will pique your interests, and you can do some searching of your own. If so, I recommend Lee Strobels's *A Case for Christ*.

I promised myself from day one that I would give you all an honest and open look at what was happening to me and what makes me tick. I believe that I have done so. I also promised God that I would never shrink from praising Him or speaking openly about Him in my blog. I believe that I have kept that promise as well.

May God bless and keep you all in His loving arms.

Your friend,
Capt. Bob

WRITTEN JUNE 11, 2010, 9:12 P.M., BY CINDY SCHULTE

Our prayers have been answered! Praise God! Bob has come out of surgery with both legs. There will be foot drop and a significant loss of bone, nerve, and muscle, but it was what we prayed for.

I want to thank all of you for your constant support with all that we are going through. I have to print this journal entry and bring it to Bob when I visit tomorrow morning so ... I will make it as newsy as possible.

Vicki, Bob, and I arrived at the hospital at 5:15 am. Bob was brought to the operating area at 6:00 with surgery set for 7:15 a.m. Vic and I spend the next ten hours learning the ins and outs of St. Francis Hospital. There is a service for people who have trouble walking. A carrier drives around picking up patients as it is done in the airport. I was offered rides because one gentleman felt I was coming in for hip replacement surgery.

The waiting room area held chairs and couches for quite a few people. One woman found it comfortable enough to snore through an hour of waiting at least. There was a phone in the room where surgeons and nurses called and updated us with information. Whoever was closest to the phone would get the name and have to call out. Because of HIPA, only first names were used. When Vicki answered, she got the easy names. Mine was Mr. Hambalinn. Ah! He didn't answer, so I hope he wasn't there. Vic did well with it and has been offered a part-time job if she is interested.

Met Mr. Pigeon-Man and spent about forty-five minutes learning the life and times of racing homing pigeons. If anyone is interested in starting a new hobby, give us a call. We can set you up.

At 7:00 p.m., we were finally able to see Bob, who is in ICU. His leg is to be immobilized for several days, and he was heavily sedated; however, he has his usual charm with the nurses. Left him at 8:00 with a wonderful nurse (Joy) and feel that he will be more alert tomorrow morning.

Thanks to Vicki, who spent the long, eventful day with me. Looking forward to the ride on the other side of surgery.

Good night.

Cindy

Written June 12, 2010, 7:31 a.m., by Cindy Schulte

Good morning! Spoke with Bob this morning, and he sounds fantastic. He's immobilized on his left side, but he sounds great despite the lack of sleep last night. A long surgery, but I am hoping he'll be able to sleep tonight. I will be up there later this morning and most of the day. He is supposed to be moved from ICU today, and as soon as I know that, I will let you all know. However, I know that as soon as he can get to reporting on his own, he will be doing it.

The one thing I failed to mention last night was my visit with the surgeon after the surgery. The surgeon came out to report the happy news that the leg was saved and the cancer removed. He showed graphic photos with such enthusiasm. I do wish that Bob could have seen this because it's right up his alley.

Please know that this will be a long comeback for Bob, but I know that God will give him the strength to get through all of this. I thank all of you for your support, and as soon as he has moved out of ICU and is taking visitors, I will let you all know.

God bless You!

Cindy

Written June 13, 2010, 9:18 p.m., by Cindy Schulte

I'm back. Yesterday was a long day with Bob being moved out of ICU into his own room (#5108) in St. Francis Hospital. I've gotten to know the hospital so well that I was able to tell the nurses that on the same floor in the ICU waiting room area, there was a soda and snack vending machine. The important things in life—food and drink. Bob is settling in for probably at least five days. If you haven't seen the Facebook page that Scott Wilcox put up, check it out. You can see how he looks. Each day, he looks better. The pain comes if he doesn't keep ahead of it, but he actually was moved into my Lili Tomlin chair. (Ah, well, it was great while it lasted!) You won't understand that unless you saw Scott's pictures of me on Facebook in a chair that was obviously made for Bob.

Each day, it's a little bit more. The braces that he will have to wear were delivered. Seems like it is moving so fast.

When I left this evening, Bob said, "I could get used to taking naps whenever I want,"

I want to send my thanks to Pastor Andy and his wonderful message today with the emphasis on the gratitude that we will offer for all the answered prayers.

Off to bed. I'll update you again.

Cindy

Written June 15, 2010, 1:04 p.m., by Cindy Schulte

Good afternoon! I believe that because I am picking up a computer to bring to the hospital today, Bob will be back. He looks great and is moving along. I expect him to be in the hospital until the end of the week and then rehab. Once he can get up fourteen stairs to get into the house (it's all one level after that), he's home free for recouping. I am also picking up a walker big enough with a seat. As for me, the commute will be better. Thanks, guys. Capt. Bob will be returning soon, and then you will get *all* the details.

God bless!

Cindy

Written June 15, 2010, 5:49 p.m.

I have a computer. I will be sending a journal out later tonight if I can stay awake for it. Much to tell you but am tired.

Praise God, and God bless you all.

Written June 16, 2010, 2:57 a.m.

Where to begin. I guess I need to beg ur forgivnrss for my typing first. I am using one of those "Netbookws" and evfery key seems to be in the wrong plsce, especisllu the punctuation keys. You are seeing the result as there is no spell-checker or pumctuation-checker on board either. My eyes are still crossed at close range, and I csn't forcus my glasses at three in the mirning on such small keys. I don't think I have a hyandle on thuis yet but I hope to go0 bacik to a laptop within a week.

I will give you my recollections since my last and hope not to clash with Cindy's, who stepped in to help me wjen I needed it most.

Operation day!

Cindy and I just said good-byes to each other, and thank you, Vicki, for being there. I told Vicki where to find my personal letter to Cindy should the operation get nasty, and now they were wheeling me to the operating room. St. Francis has twenty-six of them ... twenty-six! My gurney went through the door into a refrigerated operating theater. Wooo! "Why so cold?" I said. "Keeps down the germs," said one of the masked people. I looked around the room quickly, and it was a normal-sized room—16X24, dominated by the butcher table in the middle with lights that would make Lady Gaga blush and a huge table off to the side with what looked like a million pieces of silverware all autoclaved and ready to be slapped in the doc's hand as he yells, "Number-three scalpel please." Truly, an amazing-looking place.

I was transferred (this is what they call it) onto to the table of honor and met again all of the participants "'a sturdy bunch of children." My doctor is thirty-seven years old, and his PA is twenty-nine! Too late to stop now. The pre-op drugs feel so good.

It was time to start, and once again, we had the secret doctor-patient chat about releasing them from liability if they screw up. Go figure. Maybe a minute of quiet, and then they are ready to gas me. I thought about what I wanted on my mind when I closed my eyes perhaps for the last time, so I asked them not to make me count backward (I always hated math), and instead, I had personal things to say. As my head started to fade away, I repeated His name over and over—Jesus, Jesus, Jes—

More later.

WRITTEN JUNE 16, 2010, 7:09 P.M.

Hospitals are all about drugs. They had me on so much long-term pain drug—oxycodone 40mg—that when I took the breakthrough drug, 10mg oxycodone, I lost it and made no sense to those around me this afternoon. Sorry. Mom, Aunt Maddie, Cindy, President Lincoln, Neil Armstrong, and especially the King. Yes, Elvis was in my room today.

We all decided that 20mg of oxycodone was plenty for baseline pain, and we left the rest alone. Tomorrow, I should remember the day. I still am having problems with this small KB.

I woke up on Friday at 7:30 p.m., over twelve hours since I had gone under. I have no recollection of waking up to find my foot still attached. My day in ICU was a total washout for me—moans and pain, no movement without fire in the leg. No sickness, but needles every hour, dressing changes, bloodletting, groans, no food, incredible sweating and ultra dry mouth, swelling from the respirator ... just a terrible day. I found out later that I have a reaction to morphine that they had not counted on. Just about the time the pain is reduced by morphine, I have already passed out and forget to breath. Sleep apnea is expected to be the cause. They had to use a respirator for two-way breathing in the operating room, but the button seen on Facebook was short-lived so have been doing chemistry with the docs ever since. They have been great. Tired. More coming later, though I have a sleep test scheduled for tonight.

WRITTEN JUN 17, 2010, 4:42 P.M., BY CINDY SCHULTE

I'm back. As much as Bob would like to spend his time entering this journal, healing comes first, and as they ask him to do more, the energy leaves. So I will continue to let you know how he is doing.

I am sitting in Edith Ann's chair, writing on baby bear's computer. I think that means this is papa bear's chair.

We are finishing dinner. The news is that Bob will most likely be moved tomorrow via ambulance to Apple Rehab in Middletown. I will save on mileage there. Rehab will be long. Right now, he cannot use left leg except for balance on the walker. He will be trained on crutches but is not strong enough yet. The doctor says the skin looks good but must be watched carefully for quite a while. His stamina is low because of walking thirty feet this afternoon (not really walking ... grab walker, hold upright, hop on right foot, balance, repeat motion). But he is doing it remarkably well.

He appreciates all the cards and well-wishes (prayers ... keep 'em coming). Looks like fishing is out for this summer ... but not next year. This summer will be Apple and home. I had a railing put on the front steps to aid with his trip home. They look very nice.

Brought cherries this afternoon. They are on sale at S&S and very delicious. I checked out how to freeze them, so I am going back there.

Not much else. The pain meds were difficult for Bob as he either was out of pain but not thinking well or in pain with the need of a bit more. I think he has that figured out.

I will close here. Tough on baby bear's computer, but I just wanted you guys to get the news that he's going to rehab. Praise God.

When I leave tonight, I will listen to the game and watch it at home in my jammies. Talk to you later.

Cindy

WRITTEN JUNE 19, 2010, 4:43 P.M. BY CINDY SCHULTE

Well, it's Bob's birthday, and the party I was planning is postponed 'til he's home and can sit on the deck, watching friends and family swim in the pool. Details later.

Well ... he's halfway home at Apple Rehab. I believe we have gotten rid of the meds that did indeed produce hallucinations. I watched one yesterday while he was in the chair, waiting for the ambulance. Had to move to not get in the way of the shooting of woodchucks. The angels were offering "flows," whatever that is, and he was insistent that he get the dangerous one. Anyway, he is now on a better med and back to Bob. Phew! The facility is beautiful, and he has his own room, which I am thankful for. A bulletin board to put his cards on and a window shelf that he can put his family pictures on. He is in Room 111. Spoke to the rehab lady today, and she said that he will be busy most of the day with occupational and physical rehab. You are welcome to try to visit during the day, but after three each day is probably a good bet to miss rehabs.

Every day, Bob is gaining strength. I left him at 1:30 to rest after his evaluation, and I'm going back after supper. Hopefully, the Sox are ahead of the Dodgers after. We'll see.

That's it for today. I'll report tomorrow. Maybe now that he has gotten on better meds, he'll be entering this message. He is much better at it, but I had fun keeping you guys up on things. Thank you, Erica, for getting this whole thing started. It's been just what we needed.

C

WRITTEN JUN 20, 2010, 2:53 P.M. BY CINDY SCHULTE

Hi, guys!

I realize that I really ought to send the "CliffNotes" version of the operation so that Bob will not have to tell it all. But you can ask questions when you talk to him as he knows this better than I do.

First of all, Bob went into surgery at 7:15 a.m. Dr. S cut his left leg from the ankle to the knee (sixty staples), flipped it open to see the tumor, which was 6.5 inches in length, 5.5 inches in width, and 3 inches in depth in the shape of a turtle (which means it was tapered at the edges and the middle was the deepest). The tumor had attached to the fibula, the peroneal nerve, and one of the arteries. Hence, they were removed. The tissue was tested at 11:00 a.m. (give or take), and there was no cancer apparent. Therefore, the surgeon believes that they "got it all!" When the tumor was taken out, there was a large hole in his calf. Therefore, he took a muscle from the other side of the calf, flipped it over, and placed it in the hole to hopefully aid the skin to heal without grafts in the future. Because the fibula was taken out, the ligaments in the knee that were attached to the fibula were attached to the tibia. The flap of skin was then placed back and stapled. The surgeon was so excited about the surgery that he took pictures, and I did see them. I truly believe that this is what enables me to look at his leg now as it is healing, seeing how wonderful this job was. It will help me to help Bob as he recovers.

What we all need to know is that this surgery is extensive and the leg will need a long time to "heal" so that in the future, he will be walking. All of your prayers are asked for patience for Bob as he will need to rest as much as he can.

Thanks, guys. Sorry I didn't tell you the whole story until now. But thought it would be good to know.

Tonight I am going back to watch *Sherlock Holmes* on the computer with Bob. Should be fun.

C

Written June 21, 2010, 7:51 p.m.

Well, I am back. It's Bob at the keyboard, and I now can see only one set of keys. Last time I typed something, there were two.

I am lying here in pain. Every muscle in my legs and arms hurt, but not from the operation. Now I hurt from the physical therapy (PT). I had to do fifty reps of the easiest exercises you could imagine, like lifting a two-pound bar over your head fully extended. Ten, twenty, thirty-five, forty ... oh, my gosh, fifty. Anyway, do that to every muscle group they can isolate, and a few hours later ... pain, but a really nice pain.

I think that Cindy did a great job of filling you in on what happened on operation day. It was a miracle. I am told I spent 7.5 days in the hospital; however, I only have memories of about three and a half, and they weren't good, so let's move on.

I had access to a loaner computer over this past weekend, but security settings would only allow it to log onto Facebook, not CaringBridge. I was also very busy slapping "high fives" as many friends and family stopped in to the clinic here to celebrate and to wish me happy birthday.

I arrived at Apple Rehab last Friday via ambulance. Thank you for paying about a thousand dollars for a hot ride backward in a truck, without springs, red lights, or sirens. I found little to be thought humorous in it when it happened.

This rehab facility offers the latest in torture ... I mean, PT training, and I have made progress after only several days. I have two braces on. The largest starts at my ankle and runs all the way up to my groin. It has a metal flat bar on each side of the leg and a hinge at the knee. The hinge has been locked at 12.5 degrees, and this brace must stay on for six weeks. This brace is there to protect the three tendons that had to be moved to the tibia when the fibula was removed. I must admit that I have seen these braces in use before but never locked in one position. My mobility will be severely limited for at least six weeks. The other brace looks like a big "Après Ski" boot. My heel is firmly held into the heel of the boot, and a strap goes over my forefoot to ensure this. With that strap in place, there is one more over the toes and another around the top section about halfway up my non-calf. The whole purpose of that brace is to hold my foot at a 90 degree angle to my leg. Because I have no nerves or muscles, which used to hold that foot up, if no brace was in place, the foot would slowly fall into the pointed toe position of a ballerina dancer—I prefer not. It would be very difficult to drag that foot forward while I try to walk.

I am still changing narcotic doses each day to respond to activity level and a new pain. "Neuropathic pain" is particularly vexing and difficult to treat because there's no agreed location or physiological mechanism to target for therapy. You feel very short but sharp jolts of pain after surgery that removes nerves. In my case, early Saturday morning, the pain came while I was asleep, and I screamed into my CPAP mask. Luckily, no one will know I am such a wuss.

I am so blessed to have come through this drama so well. I still have my leg after an incredibly difficult and complex operation. While on the table, I stopped breathing because of sleep apnea, and that has been solved. I was mildly anemic and now pop daily magnesium pills. My sugar level spiked to 292; however, that was due to the invasive operation, and the body started shutting down systems (in this case, the pancreas). The sugar problem was solved by insulin, and I should be able to get off of that once my pancreas stabilizes. I received thorough physical examinations that poked into places previously unknown to the average civilized person. Everything looks good, but I found no doctor who would say I was cured of cancer. Now I will be watchful and enjoy every day that God allows me to stay on His earth.

WRITTEN JUNE 22, 2010, 8:34 P.M.

Today was spooky. I felt great when I awoke and had breakfast. I was asked to get down to the gym as soon after breakfast as possible, so I got there around 8:45 a.m. I started PT by doing fifty reps of rather easy two- to three-pound barbell moves, curls while sitting, presses, and side-to-side extended swings of the arms, and the hardest is this around-the-world maneuver where you take the bar and slowly press it down and away from you until you are extended and then slowly bring it up while fully extended to the vertical position and then back. They work on upper body strength so that they can avoid the problems that come with crutches. Apparently, if you hang on your armpits, you are in for a seriously painful experience.

Anyway, the real problem today began while I was lying down on their sports table to get my full-leg brace adjusted and it had slipped down with the activity. The hinge was two inches below the knee joint, causing pressure against the back of my non-calf. The air on the leg felt so good when they took the brace off. I asked to be allowed to just lie there, and I promptly fell asleep for twenty minutes while the rest of the class continued with knee exercises, which I did not need.

When they came back to lace up the brace, all Hades broke loose. I received a five- to six-second pain, which was the worst I had ever felt in my life. It was a shooting, white-hot knife thrust that split me wide open from my waist to my ankle. I could not control myself, and I can still hear the screams echoing down the hall. I absolutely could not believe that the noise was coming from me. The techs were not even touching me! It happened spontaneously, so I must be constantly aware of the pain's potential return. This pain occurred two more times, and each seemed worse than the former. I was starting to pass out as I was seeing stars and my head was swimming. It was awful.

I was able to let them continue to strap me up after the third round of pain. One other woman in the room was crying for me, and I was apologizing to everyone who was there. I left the gym, went back to the room, took pain meds, and called both of my doctors. The nerve pain med was doubled by the rehab center's doctor and then tripled by my surgeon. When I take the nerve pain med, I feel nothing different, no drowsiness or anything. I sure hope it works.

After a drug-induced nap and an excuse from the techs for the afternoon PT, several more friends stopped by. Thanks, Charlie, Howard, Anna, Pam, and Deb. My rock, Cindy, was there as well, but she threatened a shopping spree if I have anymore drama with the pain.

It's 8:00 p.m., and I just took another Percocet and gave orders for two more at midnight so I can sleep. More tomorrow.

WRITTEN JUNE 24, 2010, 1:33 A.M.

Today was a welcome contrast to yesterday. No phantom nerve pain, although the narcotics used to prevent it are quite strong, and my senses are dulled beyond their normal state.

Physical therapy included the normal weight-lifting stuff, but then the first big question got answered: Can Capt. Bob get into the backseat of a car for transportation? The answer is *yes*. Cindy's Subaru Forester has great big handles built into the ceiling on both sides of the rear seat. Using those plus the tops of the front seats, I was able to slide/lift myself across and belt in. I would not like to drive that way for more than about one hour max, because I am twisted a bit, but doctor's appointments are now manageable for us.

I am fortunate that under all the flubber, I have strong upper body strength from the years of working out with my gym partner, Pastor Steve. The result is that I also can handle stairs quite easily.

Using one good foot and two strong arms, I climb sixteen steps with no problem. I have ordered my carpenter to replace all of the flimsy pine rails with stronger rails, perhaps even oak, rails that are thoroughly bolted in places or at least lag-bolted into either a stud or a surface-mounted fascia board that is lagged into the studs.

My large brace on my leg has had a mechanical problem. One of the hinges that holds my leg at 15 degrees has failed and now will allow 30 degrees of movement—not good. I hope to get the device repaired or replaced tomorrow.

I have pictures of the leg and may post one on the website. What do you think? TMI or not?

WRITTEN JUNE 24, 2010, 4:52 P.M.

Short entry today. I did well again in PT and climbed eight steps today as my leg was sore from yesterday.

The infection nurse did the dressing change today, and she questioned what she was seeing with the stretched skin flap. She is of the opinion that I may have to go onto a wound/skin pump. My next doctor's appointment with the surgeon is next Tuesday morning, so key information for the blog may take that long.

Meanwhile, back at Apple Rehab, I am pretty drugged up. I am not yet hallucinating, but I talk to myself in a half-dream state all the time. I would have to say that I currently am not capable of making important decisions.

WRITTEN JUNE 25, 2010, 9:24 P.M.

All of the attention that I am getting is a heavy weight on my shoulders. It is hard for me to wrap my arms around the number of friends I have right now. I know that somewhere there is a poem that talks about having five good friends in your lifetime. I am blessed that I do have good friends in my life, and I have never relied more heavily on you. Thank you for coming through. I pray that I will be as thoughtful and concerned when some of you need reassurance.

The truth is that I am a frightened little kid right now who wants nothing better than to run into his mom's apron for comfort. Oh, how sweet those days were, bringing dandelions home for Mom and knowing that she would love them. Your cards, letters, and visits, while not able to replace my mom's apron and the hug behind it, have made my job here a lot easier. I feel that you guys believe in my ability to be healed not only from this surgery but also from the cancer.

I have spent a full week here now. The Apple Facility is half rehab and half long-term patients, and conditions here are great. Everyone, including the title nineteen patients, is cared for very well. One thing I have realized is that cards and visits mean an incredible amount to the long-term residents. While some patients are in a stupporous mode, they rise to the surface and engage when those stimulations are around.

I am just so tired. I need to sleep. Tomorrow, I shall try to climb up out of this drugged state and say something more. I love you all. May Jesus bless you all for the prayers you have offered on my behalf.

Capt. Bob

WRITTEN JUNE 27, 2010, 12:15 A.M.

Tough day today, so I am just waiting for the pain pills to kick in. My whole leg feels like it is being squeezed.

After a week, I am getting into a routine here at Apple Rehab. Routine is a good thing, as it gives one more time to think.

I think that I will forever have a different view of invalids. Now that I am one, hopefully temporarily, I can tell you that wheelchairs are fun while you are sitting still (quite comfortable) but a pain to operate. They really are quite hard to propel without a "pusher engine" like Cindy. I have a wide wheelchair (wonder why), and making turns through doorways is a rather exact science. It is pretty easy to get your hand squeezed between the drive wheel and the door. Ouch! Actually, in my case, ouch, ouch, ouch!

Walkers are another matter. They are easy to use if you really don't need one but very difficult if you do. Walkers are "transfer" tools as well as walking aids. Let's say that you were out on a hot date with your wife. Say you went to the patio for a talk and were headed back to bed for pain meds. The wheelchair gets you to the bed but will not be your vehicle of choice in the middle of the night when nature calls. It is then that the walker comes into play. But it can only come into play if you can reach it because the wheelchair is in the way. Solution: Use the chair and roll up to the walker, not the bed when you want to go to bed. Move from the chair to the walker, push the chair out of the way, and climb into bed via the walker. In this way, the walker is right where you need it when nature calls. Of course, did I mention that walkers have a downside because you have to put almost your full weight on your hands when your injury is new like mine is. Sore hands in less than three days. Weight-lifting gloves help.

Walkers are approved by weight-bearing load. Most walkers are certified for a 250-pound individual. If you know me, you know I passed 250 sometime between high school and my son's birth six years later. My walker, which is approved for a three-hundred-pound person, is like pushing a scaffold around, featuring chrome vanadium steel tubing an inch and a quarter in diameter, aircraft-quality welds, X-ray inspected to ensure durability. I won't even get into whether to get a walker with or without wheels. That is a secret that I have not yet been authorized for.

Well, in rereading this journal, I can see that I am slipping into the wonderful waters of narcotics. See you all next time I am capable of typing. Thank you for your prayers and support.

WRITTEN JUNE 29, 2010, 3:17 P.M.

It's time for another journal entry. I have more to talk about after traveling back to St. Francis Hospital to see Dr. S, my surgeon. Dr. S is the young, brilliant specialist I have been talking about in my journal entries and perhaps even in a couple Facebook status entries. He is thirty-seven years old (very young) and has accreditations far beyond his years—UConn professor, academic dean, fellow, orthopedic oncological surgeon, etc. He runs a department in St. Francis, and he was brought there to make a statement to the area that St. Francis was the place to go for this expertise. All of this happened this year. No one knows him in the area yet. I certainly didn't know him. Cindy didn't know him, but it clearly is a God thing as my first surgeon, who became concerned with the increasing complexity of the operation, did know him. When it became clear that a second opinion at a higher level of expertise was needed, I believe that God put Dr. S's name into my first surgeon's mind as a result of all of our prayers. Who has ever heard of a surgeon calling to cancel an operation on the day of the operation and then asking the patient to go for a second opinion and possibly change doctors at such a late date? It is incredible, but nothing is too incredible for God.

I found out a few things today that are helping me better understand my operation and the aftercare treatment. I think you have read my words complaining to you about my pain meds. You have heard me say, "I was out of it at times. I have lost several days. I want to cut them back." I guess I was being thickheaded as I was not listening to the doctors and nurses very well. I knew something was going on when I asked my night nurse for one Percocet tablet for a break through the pain and he brought me two. He basically said that I needed to take two because I could be hindering the healing process. What did he mean? Today, my doctor straightened me out. This eight-hour operation was an invasion into a huge part of my body. Not only did I have a skin wound over eighteen inches long, but I had also had a very large malignant tumor, a major leg artery, my peroneal nerve, and my fibula removed. After that, the surgeon moved two muscles to different locations in my leg. He took one muscle that would no longer have any use and moved it into the space where the tumor was. This was done to give the large flap of skin, which had been badly burned during my radiation phase, a blood-rich surface to try to heal on. The second muscle, which is used by the foot to push down (as in pushing down the gas peddle in a car), was moved into the previous muscle's location to maintain some type of leg symmetry. I don't have a large divot where my calf muscle was. Of course when the fibula bone was completely removed, several of its tendons had to be attached to the tibia bone, and a cadaver tendon was implanted to give stabilization to the knee. Bottom line is that the operation was eight hours long because it was a huge operation, and that is why the operation is called a "radical leg reconstruction." The doctor today told me to expect significant pain, and he was very interested in how I was holding up. When I mentioned that I was cutting back on some of the painkillers, he was not happy, as the painkillers, which I would take before the pain became unbearable, would allow the therapists to move very painful areas of the leg that are either doing new things entirely or located in places that they were not designed to be in and allow the person to get used to the idea (painfully). My cutting back on the painkillers was only going to prevent me from moving my limb that little extra distance, which could make a huge difference in my final outcome. So if you call or if you visit, you may find me in an odd state of double talk or incomplete sentences. Apparently, that will help me heal. The large flap of skin that is on top of the muscle has begun to blister, but there appears to be a redness underneath which is representative of new skin being formed. If this is true, we will avoid another operation (too scared to ask him what that operation would do). The next week or ten days should show us what we need to know about the skin flap.

Thank you so much for your prayers. God has left His fingerprints all over this illness, and I am blessed like Paul, who was knocked off his horse by God in a less than subtle encounter. I, too, have been knocked off my horse, and I am being rebuilt to do something that is not yet clear to me; however, I have a theory growing in my mind.

Now I will close and mention that I will be here in the Apple Rehab Facility for another week. Visitors are welcome but should call 860-349-3353 beforehand if possible. I usually am in therapy between 8:00 and 11:30 and again between 1:30 and 3:00.

WRITTEN JULY 1, 2010, 5:33 A.M.

The days here at Apple Rehab are a little boring and very routine. The people are great. The food is good, and the accommodations very nice. Clayton Mountain, our carpenter, called last night, and we decided on the oak banister for the staircase. He will be installing a bracket at every stud so that the strength is there. The next owners of my house can remove the brackets and sell them for scrap if they want to. I checked into the cost of wheelchairs and was surprised they are relatively inexpensive. The one I am currently using at Apple is a $400 model, and it is extra wide and heavy-duty. It is a little slow off the line, but going downhill, it gains on the others nicely. Ole Miss Budweiser took the last race, but I am looking for a rematch. Funny thing is that you do have to be somewhat careful coming out of your room into the hall while in a chair. There is a lot of activity, and it would be easy to hit someone.

The Apple building is in the shape of a boomerang. The entrance is in the center, and if you go to the left, you will find the long-term residents, while on the right, you find the rehab residents. I have gone down to the long-term resident side and visited with several to chat or to pray. It is so sad. One woman was crying in her room, repeating over and over, "It's one o'clock. He should be here. He's late." I rolled myself in, and from the door, I got her name, Mary, and spoke to her. She was distraught. After I got her to calm down a bit, I asked her who she was waiting for. She answered, "My boyfriend." She was at least eighty years old but living in a different time, waiting ... waiting. A little light banter back and forth, and I thought she might be okay, so I said good-bye. I was not yet into the hall before the crying began anew. Sad.

I met another woman sitting in her wheelchair in the hallway. She was expressionless. She neither spoke nor blinked, just stared dead ahead. I spoke to her of the weather, the glorious breezes, and the sun but got no reaction. I was at a loss as to what to do, so I just prayed out loud for her, telling her that Jesus knew every bird in the sky, every leaf on the trees, and that He certainly knew her and was waiting to see her again in heaven. I don't know if she heard me, but I had tears in my eyes as I shared that moment with her.

When they rebandage my leg daily, it looks terrible to me, but the doctors and nurses seem to see otherwise. Last night, it was bleeding lightly through a couple of the metal staples. Maybe that is normal. I don't know who to believe. I hope they are right.

WRITTEN JULY 1, 2010, 11:04 P.M.

I go to physical therapy (PT) each day. The purpose is to accomplish the following:

1. Strengthen my upper body so that I can handle a walker or crutches.

2. Enhance my balance so that I can handle issues like stumbles, tripping, etc.

3. Determine what movement I have in my leg and tone those muscles to help in my walking.

4. Get me used to dealing with what I have left.

5. Teach me the best methods for mounting chairs, walkers, beds, toilets, etc.

The sessions can run twice per day, but usually, I extend mine and finish up in a one-, two-, or three-hour session and then nap in the early afternoon. The exercises help to loosen up the arms and legs and allow movement beyond the normal range I was using prior to my surgery. There is a good amount of socializing during the PT, and everyone encourages each other. Most of the other patients have had a knee or a hip replaced. I am rolling around with two gigantic braces on my leg, so I get asked quite often what I did to earn them. Today someone asked, "What happened? Did you miss an extra point and get tackled?" It was an awkward moment when I answered that it was due to cancer.

My injury is of interest to student RNs in the building. There usually are observers in the room when my bandages are changed. My doctor's name is repeated a few times with great respect, almost as if they were praising him, and I hear comments: "Wow, it looks like a real leg." "He did a fabulous job making it look natural." I must admit that the leg may wind up looking like a "real" leg, but it sure doesn't look like one now. The skin flap is slowly blistering off as the doctor thought it might. There appears to be red tissue forming under the blisters. That would be answered prayers again. I have a doctor's appointment in Hartford next Tuesday, and we should get the official word then as to the viability of the flap. There also is the matter of about fifty staples left in my leg that need to come out. He has left them this long as they were providing some support for the primary incision and the termination of the flap. I will be glad when I get them taken out, as they are painful when I am rebandaged daily. I hate it when a new nurse does the rebandaging because they always want things to be nice and snug. When things are "snug" with my leg, they are painful. I would say that the healing of the leg could be complete as early as mid-September. By then, I hope to have the special molded brace made for my foot and be down to merely a protective covering for the leg. The skin over the shin will be extremely fragile for a while, and I may not be able to ever put that leg in the sun again. That is a small price to pay for a leg that has some functionality.

Bennett, my grandson, asked Cindy, "Will *Opa* (German for grandfather) ever move home from the hospital?" Kids don't keep very good track of days and weeks. I sure do want to come home someday soon, Bennett.

The leg is getting all the attention right now. How does it look? Will he be able to walk on it? Will it be strong enough? Look at the scars! There is an aspect that has become partially obscured while we worry about the leg itself—the cancer.

I will begin taking a lifelong series of CT scans of the chest as a follow-up for this operation. No doctor will tell you, "I got it all!" Instead, they will say, "I think I got it all!" The numbers are that 50 to 65 percent have a five-year survival rate after an operation like mine to remove cancer from a leg. My tumor was unfortunately very large, and size impacts negatively on survival rate.

Your prayers and God's intercession have gotten me this far. My conclusion is that God has more/other work for me to do with the rest of my life. I am already being drawn to do something with the American Cancer Society, and in all probability, I will do my best to collect a little money for them via one of their local campaigns. If that happens, I am afraid you may be one of the first to know about it. LOL

My stay in this nursing home has not necessarily been an eye-opener as much as it has been an affirmation. These older people need our help. As nursing homes struggle to stay in business during these tough times, their staff is being pressured to do more and different jobs. The result is that the casual conversation time between care provider and patient is almost nonexistent. What can we do about that?

WRITTEN JULY 2, 2010, 4:15 P.M.

Late breaking news!

I am to be released from Apple Rehabilitation Therapy next Thursday. My house has been prepared, and I am looking forward to getting home. More on this move and other news later.

WRITTEN JULY 3, 2010, 1:30 P.M.

Things are moving along a little more quickly now. As mentioned, I will be released from Apple Rehab next Thursday and am looking forward to returning home. I will miss some of the conveniences that Apple Rehab has to offer. No, maybe I won't miss any conveniences, as I can't think of one that I can't duplicate at home. As a matter of fact, I won't miss their four-hour schedule of vital signs, the noise in the corridors, and the 6:00 a.m. fire drill we had last week. I may miss the number of nurses they had, but the prettiest one is going to drive me home—Cindy.

I finally noticed last night that the healing is moving along nicely on the leg. Thin black skin is blistering off in favor of red growing skin underneath. There has been no infection, and we have been favoring that wound site in all things we do. I may miss my Apple bed. It was designed for burn wound victims and is comprised of twenty-one air pillows laid side by side from the foot to the head. These twenty-one air pillows are broken into three zones that have independent air pressure. The bed's small compressor is always running as the pillows have tiny holes in them near where your skin would make contact through a sheet. The air is used to dry any moistness that might harbor bacteria found in bedsores or other infections like MRSA. It makes for an interesting sleep as air is always circulating around your body under the covers. As I shift my weight while I'm sleeping, the bed firms up or softens the area I have moved to. Once we had a power outage, and in the second or two that elapsed between the power going out and the generator turning on, my bed shut itself off to protect the electronics. In a couple of minutes, I was sleeping on the plywood bottom of the bed—hard indeed. A half hour later when the main power was restored, the same thing happened, but at least then I knew to throw the reset switch on the bed.

I hope to be able to welcome some of you who might like to make a visit. Give me a call to make sure the visiting nurse is done.

Thank you for your support!

Bob Schulte

Chapter 5

Recovery

My, what a busy day this Fourth of July turned out to be! I was allowed out after all to go to church and got there shortly before 10:00 a.m. I was kept busy until 10:30, shaking hands and getting kissed by all of my prayer warrior friends at Fellowship Church. Everyone had a good word, and to my surprise, many thought that I "looked so good." I have shed about eight to ten pounds so far but didn't think that would show. The only pants that will cover my two braces are lounging pajamas, and I elected to wear my superhero pajamas that I bought for Bennett's sixth birthday party. The kids love those pajamas, and many will try to identify their favorite heroes on them. I have Captain Marvel, Spiderman, the Hulk, and several others on this pair, but one thing I don't have on them is a girl. My four-year-old granddaughter, Sadie, had a hard time understanding why there were no girl heroes on the pants. I will be shopping later this week for a pair with greater gender awareness. Whatever is the matter with these manufacturers? Don't they understand that we want to build strong women as well as men?

It was a good day to be in Fellowship. "Andy's Gang" is fixin' on leaving for the other side of the world (literally) tomorrow, and I wanted to see them all off. We will pray that they all come back safely, but I guarantee you that they will come back changed spiritually. I can't wait to see the pictures and hear the stories that they bring back.

"Rocky," the mascot for the New Britain Rock Cat baseball team, was there as well, and I had the opportunity to get my picture taken with him/it/her and my grandkids, Bennett and Sadie. Should be a good picture. Only wish that Cole and Lara could have been there so that I had a complete set of grandkids in the picture. Maybe Photoshop will be able to help.

After church, we headed back to my house where everyone went swimming (except me) and ate too much food, including me. Vicki made a great Manicotti, and for dessert, she made a chocolate cheesecake to die for. Cindy cooked up some potato fries and a red cabbage salad while grandma supplied the fruit salad and country ribs, which we barbequed. Like I said, too much food, but we ate it.

Our home had central air-conditioning installed about seven or eight years ago, but we did not treat our added room because it was to be a three-season room with no heat or air. I finally got the insulation installed in this room, and we extended the air-conditioning into this room. It has become my man-cave, and it is where I will be living for a few months while the leg heals completely.

It was fun to be home in my own house, listening to the kids enjoying the pool. I hope we have good weather later this month when my daughter, Erica, and her two, Cole and Lara, come in for a visit. We are planning a busy few days when they are here. I am already well enough to take them to the New England Air Museum (one of my favorite spots) and the Essex Steam Train and Riverboat (would get to see all my old friends and coworkers). We are working on other agenda items. If you have an idea, please mention it in the guestbook.

I was up for over six hours today, and I can feel it. My foot had an edema problem before, and it is swollen again. I will be keeping it up for the next several days.

The nurse just interrupted my journaling to change the dressings on the leg. It continues to look good with evidence of pink skin healing under the burned layer, which is sloughing off. It has been easy to concentrate on the healing process associated with the operation and the big adjustments I will be making on my mobility. In fact, I would like to continue to focus on this stage, but I really can't. At some point, I will begin to worry about the cancer. Always the cancer. Did they get it all? Not yet though. Let's decide to worry about that another time. Let's celebrate the victories to their fullest and not turn to the future yet. I have a lot of praying to do. I need to thank God for His help in getting me through this thing. I still can't believe the miracle that happened when my first specialist deferred to the second or when I had a private rebirth when I spoke to Jesus as I was going under the anesthesia. I hope to be able to write a couple of small vignettes that I might be able to present on some Sunday in the future.

Good-bye for now, and thank you for tuning in to demonstrate your continuing interest in my story.

Written July 5, 2010, 4:26 p.m.

Thank you, Nephew Ken, for calling my attention to my cell phone number listed a couple of journal entries back. I listed it incorrectly but have corrected it now. I look forward to chatting with you, Ken. Best time to get me is 9:00 a.m. until 9:00 p.m. If I am tied up in something like therapy, I will call you back.

Today was a slow day. I needed one after going home for most of yesterday and going to church and all. It is very tiring when you are not at 100 percent. Today, I learned how to use crutches, even though the trainers did not want to have me rely on that mode of transportation. I needed to know how to handle stairs with crutches, so I begged until they finally told me that I could bring in my crutches and that they would check me out. I brought in a pair loaned to me by the Prossers. The crutches date back at least twenty years and look older. The trainers were in stitches, adjusting these things for my height. I need to put new rubber ends on them if I decide to use them seriously, but they are fine for the jobs that I intend for them—short trips to the bathroom or out to check the mail. I don't plan on going hiking with them.

Today was also the day that Mary, a ninety-year-old woman, beat me in a balloon game. I was seated in my chair, and she was standing in her walker about four feet in front of me. We were batting a balloon back and forth, trying to keep it in the air. We had it going for about five minutes when my arms started to get heavy on me as I had just finished the weight-lifting portion of the PT. It was a laugh for everyone around when I cried out, "No mas." I could have gone on but was tired, but she is so much fun. She enjoyed my kidding. You had to be there, I guess. Just another funny moment at PT.

Tonight, I am the guinea pig for a nursing student named Arsi. He has done all of the preliminary exams—oxygen percentage, temperature, heart rate, etc. His next test is going to be rebandaging my wound. I wonder if he can do it. I will be walking him through every step. If he listens, he will do well as I have it down pat at this stage of the game.

Tomorrow morning is my appointment with my surgeon. I still have fifty or so staples in place, and I hope we can start to lose them. Maybe every second one. This scar is going to be a beauty. The leg itself is fairly well proportioned. His moving muscles and tendons around seemed to work pretty well. I am now standing on the leg with my full weight. I am not yet trying to walk and flex the knee. I will be waiting for permission from the doctor for that, and it will be very tentative. The crutches will help me take those first steps. Thanks, Donna and Dave.

WRITTEN JULY 6, 2010, 8:25 P.M.

Cindy and I went to Hartford this morning for a meeting with my surgeon. Dr. S examined his work and was satisfied with the healing to date, with the exception of one area that has a leathery texture and is nearly black. He is concerned that the damaged skin may be burned too deeply to allow new growth skin to form underneath. He wants to give it another week or so before he makes a decision on further action. There are two options available to us if the healing stops. First, a wound pump could be employed, and secondly, skin grafting could occur. He removed about ten to fifteen staples (ouch).

Dr. S had some good news. The tumor was examined in the lab, and the negative margins were greater than 2mm and were clean of cancer cells. This official report supported the "quick examination" done during the operation. The leg should take from ten to fourteen weeks to heal if all goes well.

After our Hartford trip, we headed back to the nursing home, and Cindy picked up some Dunkin' Donuts coffee and a couple of snacks. It was good to relax in an air-conditioned room with the coffee.

WRITTEN JULY 7, 2010, 4:31 P.M.

My stay at Eagle Healthcare in Middletown is ending tomorrow. I will be checking out of here at 10:00 a.m.

I will be taking with me a rather complicated assortment of treatment history reports as well as scripts for all medication, which will give me enough medicine to get me through until my next doctor's appointment. I will also have orders for workers in the home to provide: occupational therapist, physical therapy, a home health aide, and a visiting nurse to change the dressings daily. My brand new wheelchair will be shipped to arrive tomorrow afternoon as well. I cannot imagine what President Obama's new health-care program is going to do better than the program I have. I for one am very glad that this cancer occurred now as opposed to later.

Thank you for being there for me. Your support has been an important ingredient to my success so far. Please keep up the prayers and include Ken Berril in your prayers. He had a heart transplant and has spent twenty-one weeks in the Hartford Hospital in the same room. He is in Apple Rehab now and is fighting to maintain his independence.

WRITTEN JULY 8, 2010, 10:55 P.M.

Home at last, home at last. Thank God Almighty I am home at last.

All you have to do to appreciate your own home is to be forced to leave it for a month. Coming home is sweet! Getting home was a riot. Thank you, Jeff, for the assistance in getting up and down the stairs and over the rough terrain. No thanks, Toyota, for ringing the seatbelt warning all the way home because we loaded a few items on the front passenger seat.

I am settled in to my new digs at home! Cindy has set up a bedroom for me in the "man-cave." Everything a guy could ever need— comfortable bed raised to manly height, TV, remote control, air-conditioning, bottled water, and a urine bottle that gets magically emptied.

My wheelchair was delivered with the wrong leg extensions, and in fact, the chair was the wrong size for my size. They shipped a mamma bear chair for a papa bear chair that felt like a baby bear chair. A special order was entered, and we get the correct one in five to seven workdays.

Cindy has just informed me that "we" have a busy day tomorrow. I said, "How can that be? I am bedridden." Here is the list: Vicki, Bennett, and Sadie are coming over to swim. Yay! Vicki is leaving the kids with us while she picks her sister up from the train station. Yay, yay! Beth is coming from Texas to visit. Yay, yay, yay! My wheelchair leg extensions for the wrong chair are being delivered. Boo! My RX pain meds have to be picked up at the pharmacy. Yay! Pick up last-minute food from Durham Market. Yay! Call Home Health Services to work out nursing services schedule. Boo! Call Apple Rehab to pick up clothes we forgot on the back of the bathroom door. Boo! Air-conditioning guys are installing our back-ordered grate for the vent. Yay! Mary is stopping by with a walker for downstairs. Yay! Marge and Al are visiting and bringing dinner. Yay, yay, yay! Clayton, our carpenter, is putting up the new railings in the stairwell. Yay! Okay, so there are more yays than boos, but a logistical nightmare!

Debbie spent the afternoon with us and cooked us a wonderful chicken dinner. Afterward, we finally finished the *Sherlock Holmes* video Vicki gave me for my birthday. It is a crazy movie that redeems itself at the end. It was a dark, dark movie. Looks like there may be a sequel by the way it ends. Moriarty is still out there!

WRITTEN JULY 9, 2010, 11:51 P.M.

Wow, what a day!

It was busy around here, but overall, it was a great first day at home. I may have pushed it a little bit, but not to bad. When I push the leg, it barks back pretty good for a while; however, the meds calm it down, and life goes on.

We did accomplish all of the items listed in last night's journal. I will comment on a few of the more interesting ones.

We had our first visit from Middlesex Hospital's Visiting Nurse Program. A nurse manager came out to the house at about 12:15

today and stayed until 2:00. She basically set the program up based on her expertise, and she will type up procedural documents for the regular nurses to follow. For instance, she documented exactly how my leg needed to be bandaged, and each nurse will follow those instructions.

I have been set up for daily visits by nurses for a while, with my wife, Cindy, looking on, so she may bandage at some point in the future. We are authorized for a home health aide, but with VNs every day, there is no point to having that duplication. I would guess that the VN arrangement will run into early August unless we have to resort to the wound pump for healing the badly burned area of the wound. Then it could be extended.

I will be evaluated by someone for occupational therapy (OT) and physical therapy (PT). A plan will be written for me for these two services. I enjoyed these at the nursing home, so I look forward to it at home. A five-pound weight doing seventy-five reps can bring up a nice mild sweat and builds long elastic muscles. I feel stronger after three weeks of it.

The railings were installed in the stairwell tonight, and tomorrow, they will be finished, polyurethaned and reinstalled when dry. They look rugged.

My undersized wheelchair now has its leg extensions installed, and the correct wheelchair is on order. At least I have something for church on Sunday. The VN suggested that I not go to church yet, but when I told her that I already went with permission from the nursing home last Sunday, she changed her mind.

Beth got in from Texas safely today and is enjoying her nephew and niece. Sadie and Bennett will be over in the morning to try out the pool with her, weather permitting.

WRITTEN JULY 12, 2010, 1:46 A.M.

Here are some random things that seem important.

My recovery continues. I am still kind of amazed with what was done to my leg. Sometimes it's hard to believe it really happened to me. I think the mind does funny things to maybe protect itself. The reality and the complexity of the operation and what was done are concepts that are coming slowly. From the left knee down, nothing is "as standard issue." It is all very perplexing. I really don't know what to think. I am not in distress or anything, but it's hard to wrap my arms around this whole event and make much sense of it. It all began just about six months ago with a small bump on my leg that did not hurt or bother me until a month or so later. Now I am extremely lucky to have a leg at all.

I do believe that God has stepped in to give me more direction in life, which I needed. I don't feel different, but I do sense a change in the way I feel about people and nursing homes. As most of you know, Cindy and I were working on organizing the Fellowship Church Care Team, and little did we know that one of the first church members that would benefit from it would be me/us. We have been blessed to have many visitors and gifts of food, which are so appreciated when the day is filled with so many busy tasks associated with my illness. I want to repeat myself because I don't think that a normal person can fully comprehend the importance of a friendly hand, a smile, a dish of food, or a fervent prayer. Only after you are on the needing side of the arrangement can you understand the importance of it.

God built us to be social beings. He invented family, and nothing gives me more pleasure than participating with my family. I can enjoy myself alone. I never get bored, but put me around family, and I enter a blissful place where satisfaction seems to engulf me. Yesterday, Vicki, Rich, and the grandkids came over for the day. I don't now if they planned to spend the day, but that is what happened. Rich's brother, Bill, came over, and Beth is visiting from Texas. Everyone played in the pool. I could hear them. I could prop myself up on my hands and peek out the window and see them, but I was upstairs in bed apart from them. That didn't matter. Memories were being made yesterday. Bennett and Sadie had a great day with their parents, uncle and aunt, and Meme (grandma). I could only dream of similar days that I had spent with my own parents at a lake where we spent vacations during my own childhood. I was excited for the kids. When the rains came and chased everyone away from the pool and into a lunch mode, I was talking to Bennett, and I asked him if he had had a good time. He was very excited and happy and had that special, beaming smile that he gets, with his fists clenched up by his eyes just like Vicki did when she was a kid. I asked him to remember the day so that when he was older, he would revel in those wonderful memories as I had with my own childhood. I asked him to remember me. We talked about special times, and I asked him to always remember the fun we have when we go fishing. He understood what I was saying, and Bennett stunned me when he said, "Opa, I will always think of you whenever I see the woods because of all the hikes that we have taken." I can't describe what I felt at that moment. My heart just melted for this sensitive boy who expresses his love so wonderfully. I have to confess that I teared up big time when he said that. What more can a grandpa ask for?

My other two grandchildren, Cole and Lara, are coming into town next week for four or five days. They live in Minneapolis, and because of the distance, I do not get to see them very often. In spite of that, I am amazed how fast we spin our relationship back up to speed when we are together. Their parents are wonderful parents, and these two kids reflect that upbringing in their interest in life, family, and relationships. Lara looks at me with those probing eyes, and in all seriousness, she can ask a question that blows my mind. No fast answers here. Think before you speak. Her heart is open wide. Use the brain, Opa. Cole must be the kid they modeled the TV show *Are You Smarter than a Fifth Grader* after. I am talking seriously smart, with a complex mind that is difficult for many to follow. He is the chess player that is thinking five moves ahead at all times. I know I am bragging here about my grandkids, but I am also just telling the truth. The kids of today are amazing, and I have four grandkids who make me proud in so many ways beyond the norm. My grandkids are already good people.

Okay, enough of that. Sorry for the huge tangent. Back to cancer. Oh my, what a lovely subject. Let's not talk about cancer tonight. Tonight, I am cancer-free. Good night, Moon.

WRITTEN JULY 14, 2010, 12:42 A.M.

No matter what I say or do, the days keep passing by. I now have an assortment of visiting nurses and therapists assigned to work with me. (You may substitute the word "bother" for the word "work" in the last sentence.) I have had five visits since I got home, and not one has been from the same person. I now can recite from memory my entire medical history, including Latin words, dates, and medications. I hope Mary, Dorothy, David, Kim, and Susan are now happy. We cancelled the "home health aide" before she/he showed up. We could not see the need.

We had my weekly doctor's appointment today in Hartford, and he is satisfied with the healing that occurred this past week. The wound is about fifteen inches long and consists of radiated and non-radiated skin. The skin that was not burned has almost completely healed while the area of radiated skin, which is about eight to nine inches long by 1.5 to two inches wide, remains heavily crusted over. This area will have the worst scarring, if it heals at all without skin-grafting. I would like it to be left alone and not have to go in for a grafting procedure. I have no intentions of entering a bathing beauty contest where leg shape will make a difference. The doctor took out another ten to fifteen staples today, about every other one, and my leg brace has been adjusted to allow 90 degrees of movement at the knee. Originally, it held me to 15 degrees of movement. Then last week, 60 degrees and now 90. I would love to get rid of the brace completely, but it does protect the wound, so it probably will stay on for a couple more weeks.

My new wheelchair has arrived. It fits me well and has leg rests that telescope far enough to get my left leg up on the rest comfortably. I have two walkers that I can use in the house, one per floor, crutches for shorter excursions outside (to the doctors), and the wheelchair for things like church. I can navigate only about fifty feet with the walker before exhaustion kicks in and I need to sit. The same happens for the crutches after about a hundred feet. The wheelchair, which has become my friend, is the only mode of travel for me that I can sustain for any reasonable length of time or distance.

I am now placing 100 percent of my weight on the left leg, but I cannot take more than a half step with it. In the walker or on crutches, I have an uncomfortable gait consisting of half a step with the bad leg followed quickly by the good leg. It is a stunted gait and very tiring. I am not complaining. As a matter of fact, I am bragging as no one thought that I would be doing this well so soon. A couple of the visiting nurses were very interested to see the result of such a complex leg operation. I am still overwhelmed with the fact that it took eight hours on the operating table. The doctor seems to shrug it off as "all in a day's work." I think he actually liked having to do the operation because it was a challenge and something to be proud of. He took many pictures as he worked, and I will be getting a full set at some point after this thing is healed.

Our many friends from the community and from church continue to pray and provide us with food. Breakfast is the only meal that we actually prepare. Tonight, Richard and Barbara brought over a great sweet-and-sour meatball and noodle meal followed by a great apple pie. We have some leftovers for lunch tomorrow! Thank you, guys!

God has had His hand in this from the beginning. He continues to watch over us both through our friends and community. Cindy and I are humbled and deeply awed by this whole experience. I would not trade it for the world. I feel like St. Paul, knocked off my horse and spoken to by God. I needed just that in my journey with God. Never again in those deep dark moments when the evil one is talking to me will I ever doubt the existence of my redeemer. I feel as though the Holy Ghost has taken a residence in me. I don't deserve it, just as I don't deserve salvation, but the free gift of my redeemer king has reconciled me with God. Oh, what a wonderful feeling it is to know the truth!

Clayton, our carpenter, has finished the handrail upgrade in the house. It was a much bigger job than I had anticipated. He put in about twelve hours in labor. The result is beautiful and strong. Now Cindy and I will always have strong handrails on both sides of the stairs. I was able to lightly sand and finish the top surface of the handrails in an attempt to help out and contain costs. You should have seen the process. I had to start at the bottom of the stairs, holding on to the opposite rail while I worked my way up to the second floor of the house, once for sanding, once for wipe-down, and finally for polyurethane. I was nearly in a faint when I was done, but my Schulte hardheadedness would not let me fail in this little job. By the way, I would not do it again.

Well, that is it for now. I hope I am not boring you too much, but I have been encouraged to continue to share my journey. This healing side of my cancer is coming along nicely by my way of thinking. The threat of a reoccurrence of cancer will always be there, and the doctor and I have already had some discussion on using a plan of alternating CT scans with X-rays every three months. The amount of radiation that was delivered to my leg is near the maximum lifetime allowable by good medical practice.

Good night again.

Written July 14, 2010, 5:38 p.m.

Today was the closest thing to a normal day that I have had in a while.

Mary, the head visiting nurse, was here around noon with a student, and she changed the bandage using supplies that had been ordered through my insurance company. I get along well with her, and we worked out a few things relative to our bandaging schedule next week. Tuesday is going to be my busy day next week as I have blood tests, a doctor's appointment, and a magical mystery tour with my grandchildren planned.

I met with Karen, the Democratic registrar, in my home this afternoon. Primary Day, August 10th, is a busy day for us as we run the primary vote, which will designate who will actually be campaigning for the November election in Connecticut. I am the Republican registrar for the town of Durham. Karen and I make a great team as politics does not enter into our work at all. We leave all of our opinions out on the street when we do this job to ensure that every voter has a safe environment to cast the vote of his or her choice. Staffing for primaries is different than staffing for election, as each candidate in the primary is allowed to request specific people to work the polls. We as registrars have final decision on the matter, and it is important to us that our own regular poll workers man the positions of importance so our count is perfect while we allow the candidates' choices to oversee the operation so that they are satisfied with our accuracy. My first day back as registrar looks like it will be a registration session we will have in a local nursing home. I will be very at ease in my own wheelchair. I love working with the older residents of these homes as they usually love to share their histories and much can be gained by us if we listen carefully to these people.

Yesterday, my doctor reduced the amount of painkiller I am taking. I seem to be doing okay today, but I can tell the difference. My leg is yelling a lot more, but it is tolerable. Everyone is walking around me, asking, "What number is your pain now on a scale of one to ten?" The only ten pain that I have had was the sharp nerve pain that I experienced with the trainers at Apple. Today, my pain at worst was a four. I usually start to medicate at four, but today, I decided to go to five before I took something. When medicated so that my pain is at zero, my cognitive brain activity is zero as well. What a laugh. Neat thing is that when people call and say something about a conversation I had with them a week ago, I have a great excuse for saying, "I don't remember." Indeed, I did have a couple of days in the hospital where I forgot people who came in to see me. My mother-in-law was one! I hope I don't have to pay for that mistake for too long.

I wonder if any of you reading this blog have any questions that you would like answered from my point of view. If you do, please post it as a guestbook entry, and I will have a "go" at it as they say in Australia.

This was added at 10:20 p.m. Clayton came over with his fancy new digital camera, and I spent about an hour fooling with it. Nice unit—Olympus Stylus 8010 Tough. Waterproof to thirty-three feet (one atmosphere) and drop proof to six feet. Fourteen megapixel—wow. All this activity brought the hurt level up on the leg quite a bit, but with an hour's rest, it settled down nicely. I think that is progress without pills. Brad, nice to hear from you. I would love to chat.

WRITTEN JULY 15, 2010, 1:41 P.M.

Thursday: Today, I had my first in-home PT. I should have kept it up on my own after the rehab, but anyway, I am back into it with therapist Sandy's assistance. I was sure that I wanted to cancel PT entirely as a part of my home care, but after I worked with her today, I was incredibly impressed with her knowledge of the human body and more specifically, what I can expect and cannot expect my new reconstructed leg to do. She is an extremely informed therapist and fun to talk to. She is a triathlete and has run both the New York and Boston marathons with a personal best of just over three hours, so her PT suggestions are based on personal experience as well as book learning. Sandy gave me great suggestions, and I will see her again after Erica and the kids leave next week.

Mary, my visiting nurse, just left at 1:40 p.m. My leg is all ready for another day. Mary is a very busy nurse, and I realized that she was also bandaging Peter, a friend of mine who inserted an arm into a rototiller's business end—not good—but he was lucky and is recovering. The plan is for Cindy to learn the fine points of my dressing change on Friday and do it for me over the weekend.

Note: Insert almost twenty hours of sleep at this point.

It is the next day, and I don't know what happened to me. Yesterday afternoon, I became very tired and started to sleep. I would sleep for a while and then come back up to a semi-awake stupor for a little while and then sleep again, down, down into what felt like a drugged sleep (without the drugs). We had a dinner get-together scheduled for last night. The dinner was for Cindy and me, Bennett, Sadie, Clayton Mountain, and his two kids, Ashley and Justin, and finally Scott from church. I was told that the kids were noisy, playing piano in the other room, and I slept right through dinner and all the noise. I woke up later and had a short visit with Scott and then slept through the night. I awoke this morning, rested and alert. Does anyone know what happened to me? Did my body just shut down from need of sleep? I had been active before, but I didn't think I was overly tired?

So it's today, Friday, and I have just finished my sponge bath and am waiting for yet another visitor. This time, it will be the OT guy, occupational therapist. He plans to show me how to put on a sock and take a shower. I am not sure that he will have a very interested subject because I already can put on my socks (I call Cindy) and I am not allowed to shower yet unless I change bandages at the same time, something he can't do. I kind of like the sponge baths. Cindy does my back, and it always feels so good. I don't know why I didn't start taking baths this way a long time ago.

Lee and Dianne from Charlotte sent me a beautiful card and a small book titled *Facing Illness with Hope: Leaning on Jesus*. It is a marvelous little book for people with serious illness. I found one little prayer that particularly comforted me and would like to share it with you"

> "I'm hurting Lord. I admit it.
> I'm scared and confused
>
> So I am asking you to remember,
> to remember all those promises
> you gave in your word.
>
> Help me to remember those promises.
> I'm relying on them.
> They've given me hope in the past,
> and I need to hold tight to them now.
> They will revive and comfort me.
>
> I know you won't forget me, Jesus.
> I remember with you there is hope—
> not a wishful hope—a certain hope.
> Hope for the here and the now.
> Hope for my future.
> Hope as I face this challenge,
> leaning on you and your promises."

WRITTEN JULY 17, 2010, 7:15 P.M.

Just a short note to tell you that I am feeling better and have more energy again. I think Pam had it right when she said I had tackled too much too soon.

I am enjoying my air-conditioned home but realize that I will be missing an entire summer with this illness. I am dealing with a little fleeting depression, which I was told to expect from the high dose of Neurontin that I am on. It is a pretty sneaky depression but not severe enough for me to have to hire a clown.

I hope all my friends on CaringBridge and Facebook are enjoying the weather with swimming activities or at least boating. My boat sits in my garage.

See some of you in church tomorrow.

WRITTEN JULY 19, 2010, 7:11 P.M.

It has been about two days since I wrote in my journal, and the report is positive.

Sunday: I was able to get to church, and my friend Pastor Steve from South Carolina was the guest preacher today. His was a good message, and he and I had a few friendly words back and forth in a kidding way. I have learned never to tell him something that you want to keep quiet. He always would mention it from the platform on the next Sunday. It was a riot when he was here.

After church, Cindy and I came home, and she got the house ready for my daughter, Erica, and my two grandchildren to come for a visit on Monday. Cindy really worked hard and ended the day by going food shopping at 9:00 p.m. Yuck!

Monday: Erica and the kids got in safely from Minneapolis and arrived in Hartford around noon. Cindy picked them up at the airport. We had a pool party in between thunderstorms today, and the kids had a ball playing with Bennett and Sadie, who were here with us today.

I was able to get down to the pool and sit in the shade to watch the action. A barbeque this evening finished off a busy day for me, but I did not push myself. Tomorrow is a big day—blood tests, a doctor's visit and then the Aviation Museum in Hartford. I hope the doctor is going to allow me to take one of these braces off. It's still crutches, walker, or wheelchair for me, but I can hobble a few steps with great unease and lack of balance.

WRITTEN JULY 20, 2010, 4:42 P.M.

Today was tiring. First stop at the Quest Lab for blood tests, then the surgeon's for my weekly exam, and then on to the Air Museum at Bradley Field for the four grandchildren.

What can I say? It was their day, and I tried to keep up in my wheelchair but finally just stopped and watched from afar. The Air Museum is a great day, and they had a live presentation by the man who flew a helicopter over the Atlantic to Scotland for the first time in 1952. This retired officer won the Distinguished Flying Cross for his fifty-two missions as a pilot of a B24 in Europe and then stayed in the service through Korea and finally this epic flight in 1952.

The doctor liked what he saw and thinks I will be a couple more months in healing completely. He took out the last of the fifty-two staples today. The leg is not pretty, but it is there!

I am wiped out by the activity and now enjoying a much needed rest.

WRITTEN JULY 22, 2010, 10:51 P.M.

One thing I promised myself from the start of this journaling was that I was going to be honest with you. Through all of the hospitals and the rehab center procedures and the pain, I have told it like it was, and you guys have been great.

I said the above because I am dealing now with a problem that is more mental than physical, and it is embarrassing to me to mention it, as I guess I would like to continue to think of myself as stronger than most or as a role model for someone who is going through health trials.

The bottom-line, honest statement that I want to make is that I am dealing with depression like nothing I have had to deal with before. My emotions are on the surface, and a friend walking into the room has a good chance of seeing me cry because I am so glad for the diversion or overwhelmed by the visit. I hope that it is the Neurontin medication as it does say that people taking heavy doses (over 1800mgs per day) can become very depressed while on it and they could even think of suicide. (Don't worry. I am not there yet.)

Please pray for this feeling to leave my mind. I want to continue to be the "class clown" that I have been my whole life. It fits me.

Physically, the surgeon is satisfied with the healing to date. He is optimistic that he got all of the cancer. I wish I knew him better so that I could read if he just says that to all of his patients. Coming into this thing, I knew I had a fifty-fifty chance of survival. Unfortunately, it will take me five years to find out in which half of the class I stood. It is becoming less likely that I will need skin-grafting as my body is healing the radiated skin slowly. He thinks it will be ten to fourteen weeks before the healing is complete. I walk with a walker for maybe fifty feet and then must sit. Crutches, a bit further, but when I get tired, I start to lose it and am afraid of falling. The wheelchair works with pushing help. I wheeled myself around one day this week and really experienced fatigue in my arms for twenty-four hours afterward. I have a new appreciation for people who are disabled.

Sorry to complain like this, but I feel as if I can talk to you in this journal and you will understand where it is coming from. I have not even been able to talk as openly about this in person. I hope I don't regret this honesty tomorrow.

I am going to talk to Jesus for a while now and see what He wants to reveal to me about this. I am not afraid of dying, but boy, the sickness that happens just before and what happens to my wife bothers me. Even in her own battle with MS, Cindy has been superhuman in dealing with my needs. I really did marry up.

My prayer for you is that you will remain healthy, be loved by many, and die with your shoes on after you have developed a relationship with the King, Jesus Christ. Good night, all.

WRITTEN JULY 23, 2010, 8:10 P.M.

I am very touched by the immediate response I received from last night's journal entry. I suggest that you all read the guestbook entries if you have not been doing so, as people have come back to me with incredibly personal and appropriate suggestions.

Thank you for sharing some of your own pain and how you have dealt or are dealing with it. I feel as if I have been heard by people I love and people who understand life and Bob Schulte. I am grateful to you all. Today was better. I am studying Psalm 139 and finding statements within it that apply to me and that encourage me to trust in the ever-present Lord in everything I do.

I believe in "spiritual warfare," and I believe that the evil one has been trying to break my spirit during my weakness. Your suggestions will better prepare me for the battle we all face as believers in Christ the King.

A special shout-out to Beth, who lost her husband just about two weeks ago and still had time to send me a very beautiful guestbook entry. I can't wait to see the travel log. I hope both of you enjoy that trip, as Richard is with you in spirit. Love, peace, light to you, Beth.

WRITTEN JULY 24, 2010, 9:21 P.M.

The past forty-eight hours have been a learning experience for me.

As I sank into my own depression, I wasn't thinking about others. I was completely focused on myself, and I was feeling pretty much out of control and sorry for myself. Several of you wrote guestbook entries sharing your own stories of depression with all of us. Others wrote e-mails that were quite detailed and profound about how they dealt with their own demons.

Pastor Andy stopped over unannounced as well and shared Psalm 139 with me. My take on the theme of 139 is that God has been with us since our forming in the womb and that He will be with us always in everything we do. One friend offered praise to God for everything that he received, both good and bad. Can you thank God even for the bad things that happen? That is a tough thing for most but something that finally raised one writer from his depression.

My nighttime prayer is this:

Father God, Jehovah Rafa, God and healer of the sick, I praise Your name and ask to learn how to praise you more, for Your very presence in my life. John the Baptist said, "Christ *must increase,* and I *must* decrease." Lord, I strain against such a statement as I am imperfect and proud. Help me to better understand John's words, help me to become more of a backdrop for Your perfection. I ask that You give me understanding to realize better how You are working in my life and in the lives of those around me. Please, oh, Lord, continue to bless our church and thank you for letting us witness wonderful things being accomplished not by our works but by Your love and the blood on a simple wooden cross on that wonderful day on the hill overlooking Jerusalem. Finally, Lord, thank you for Your gift of grace.

WRITTEN JULY 25, 2010, 9:54 P.M.

Today was a day of disappointment and of joy.

Everything started out just okay. I had taken my first bath yesterday and must wait several days between for healing concerns. I didn't feel too perky but was looking forward to church at 10:30 a.m. I got up out of my bed to clean up at about 9:00 and felt light-headed, not quite right. I did make it to the bathroom with my walker but really had to sit down and put my head between my legs. I was going to faint. I sat there a bit and realized that this light-headedness was not going to leave, so I called Cindy and asked her to get our carpenter, who happened to be working here today, to come in. By this time, I was short of breath and wanted to be sure that I had someone who could let me down if I fainted. I knew what was happening, I have atrial fibrillation, and I was having an episode. Clayton got me back to bed, and I doubled up on my morning med, Rythmol, which is used to control my heart when it roars out of control. Typically, my heart will go to about 100 to 110 beats per minute, and if you listen to my heartbeat, you instantly know that there is no "lub-dub" about it. Instead, you might hear something that sounds more like a tap dance than a heart in sinus rhythm.

The meds worked, and by 11:00 a.m., I was back to normal. We had almost made the decision to go to the emergency room when the heart calmed down and all was better.

I missed church, which was my one planned social event of the day. Cindy and I then decided that we would take it easy and work on thank-you notes to some of the people who have really been supporters of us through my illness. One note got done. Cindy wrote, and I dictated as my handwriting is slow and poor. Then the phone started ringing—political recordings from candidates that think I am going to listen to their balderdash and then a couple from friends who wanted to visit. Cindy and I love visits and feel renewed afterward. Steve stopped over with baked stuffed peppers (they were absolutely fabulous for dinner, Steve) and two boxes of ammunition that I could not find in my local gun store. We had a nice visit, and I look forward to spending more time with Steve and his expecting wife and daughter.

A short nap later, our "adopted" sister Deb arrived, and we had a long, slow-moving, low-key afternoon and evening. She just left after we had watched a few videos done by "Jesus Culture." We all love Kim Walker. What a voice.

Tomorrow, we get to care for Bennett and Sadie. We will not need any social planning for tomorrow. Sadie will handle that. Maybe a MMT (magical mystery tour). We will see.

WRITTEN JULY 27, 2010, 9:32 P.M.

Had an appointment with my surgeon, Dr. S today.

It was an important day for me as I am officially allowed to remove my full-leg brace. (Actually, I took it off last Wednesday and told the doctor today I wasn't going to wear it anymore. I didn't even bring it with me to the doctor's office.)

They changed the bandage and have decided that I need to go to a "wound center" at St. Francis, where they will attempt to facilitate healing by removing eschara from the dead, radiated skin and allow new healing to come in from the sides and bottom. (In lay language, they are going to peal back the scab, which is about an eighth of an inch thick, and let it heal again.) My only prayer is that they deaden that area before they start stripping the scab back. Oh and by the way, I will be looking in the other direction for this one.

My stamina is improving greatly each day. I actually was up in a vertical position of one sort or another, walking and sitting for about eight hours today, and I worked for two hours in town hall. I started the day on crutches and a wheelchair and ended it using a cane only! I still am one step at a time and fairly slow, but I am starting to get some balance back!

I still have to wear the short foot brace to hold my foot up, and the edema (swelling) on the foot is pretty bad still; however, the swelling does not seem to be related to walking or sitting. It is just swelling related to the operation, and it should go down. As soon as the swelling does go down, I can have my final molded brace made, and I can start to wear shoes again. When I can wear shoes again, watch out world. *I will be mobile,* and many of you will have a visitor!

I am in a much better mood than I was a week ago as I can see progress now and I am getting much stronger.

I have made the decision to close "Computer House Call," and I already have curtailed my captaining activities. I owe my oldest friend of over sixty years a visit in California and plan to vacation somewhere that "I want to go" next spring or summer. One of the places that I would like to go to is Katmandu so that I can fly over Mt. Everest in Nepal. I just have not figured out how to get there by boat. I still don't fit in airplane seats, especially for long flights like that.

Al and Marge gave me a book when I first went into the hospital, but I could not read in the hospital or in the rehab center. I don't know why, but my eyes couldn't focus. (Pain meds maybe?) In the middle of my depression last week and in an effort to get my mind off the crazy thoughts I was having, I picked up the book again. It is a true story of life and death titled *90 Minutes in Heaven* by Don Piper. I cannot tell you how perfect that book is for someone in a depressed state. I think that God fixed it so I didn't read it until I really needed it. Seriously, if you know of someone that is seriously ill, this book is for them.

I hope that today is an indication of the progress that I will be making now. The wound center won't set me back. It will just mean that I will have bandages on my leg for a while longer. I don't think that it will slow me down.

I got a nice guestbook entry today from Bob at the valley railroad, and he knows that I want badly to take a ride on M/V Becky Thatcher. Bob, if you're listening, I am thinking of mid-August for a day on Becky—all trips, just enjoying the ride, the people, and of course, the wonderful Connecticut River. I will call you and BB so that I may stop into the office beforehand.

There is one more thing that I need to say. My wife, Cindy, was concerned about her nursing abilities. I want to go on record right now to say that she has been a blessing to me. She has never once lost her patience with me (an almost impossible thing to do!) and has learned all the things necessary to change my dressings, handle and collate my meds, help me with really personal stuff, and feed me to boot, all this while cleaning house, paying the bills, and listening to Linda McMahon's telephone calls. She truly is a trooper, and I am delighted in her new abilities shown during this illness.

I know that I am rambling. Sorry, but I have been busy today, and I had a lot to say.

Here's tonight's prayer:

Heavenly Father, I thank You for hearing my prayers and the prayers of so many that know You. I pray that others who do not have a personal relationship with You might feel a little jealous of the miracle that You have done in my life. You have saved my leg so that I may serve others in need. You put me in a wheelchair so that I could approach nursing home patients as equals. I thank You for that insight. Thank You for the surgeon's skill and for Cindy's care. Thank You for the pain so that I now know what it is to be painless. Father God, if it is Your will, I pray that the cancer is totally gone and that it will not return. God bless each and every one who reads this prayer today, Lord. In Jesus's name, I pray. Amen.

WRITTEN JULY 29, 2010, 12:35 A.M.

I did fairly well on the cane alone today. By evening, I was unsteady on my feet as some of the balance was gone. I was just tired because after resting a bit, it got better.

The doctor on Tuesday okayed my driving, and today, I took a easy ride back to Apple Rehab (nursing home) that I stayed in for those three weeks of PT and OT immediately after the operation. I have many friends there, and I got quite a welcome back when I arrived. I wanted to share with them a simple device that my visiting therapist gave me to borrow for exercising the muscles in the hand and wrist. It was made by taking an eighteen-inch piece of three-quarter pipe and putting bicycle handgrips on either end. Then you drill a small hole right through the pipe in the middle and attach a strong cord. We call it "small stuff" on the boat. Make the line about four feet long and attach a weight of say three pounds to the loose end of the line. The exercise is completed by winding the weight up to the bar with your hands on the handle grips. Sounds easy, doesn't it? I guarantee you that winding it up and lowering it five times will give you a burn that you can't forget. It is an awesome way to strengthen your hands so that jars are easy to open again.

I visited with a couple of the patients I know just to say hello and then enjoyed an hour of music and singing with them in the rec room. I am looking forward to having a care team meeting at this home on August 11th, and I am looking for care team members to attend. I will be e-mailing particulars out to our team members next week.

The Red Sox won again today, so all is happy in our house. We now have the Yankees right where we want them (eight games ahead) for our run at the American League East Crown!

WRITTEN JULY 30, 2010, 3:20 P.M.

I changed the style of this website today. I searched for the correct ribbon color for "malignant fibrous histeocytoma" but came up short, so I went with lavender, which is a "general cancer awareness" color.

I still have a hard time saying that I am a two-time cancer survivor. It is so surreal. God is slowly making me more aware of all that has happened one bit at a time, probably because He knows what I can handle in one bit. Cindy and I stopped by the Apple Rehab Center, where I stayed for three weeks. When I left, I wrote a complimentary letter to upper management, and when we returned, several people mentioned it, as it flowed downhill to the workers. I am amazed to tell you that I just barely remember writing the well-deserved letter. I realize now that even in the rehab center, I was pretty well drugged up—functional but drugged. Small things and many kindnesses from you are only now coming back. Very sobering.

I just want to mention something else. Cindy is cooking tonight. It's the first time since my operation that we are not eating from food brought to us or prepared for us in our home. I am not suggesting here that everyone run out and get sick so you can eat well, but I am stating that in our church, we have people who go out of their way to help those in need. We have done that in the past for others, but we have never been on the receiving end. Please believe this: You will never understand the wonderful gift that food is until you receive it. We are profoundly grateful.

WRITTEN JULY 31, 2010, 1:13 P.M.

(There is graphic content in this entry. Read at your own risk.)

I guess some things you just can't rush. I have been feeling stronger these past few days, so I exercised a little more aggressively yesterday. The visiting nurse gave me a strip of "Thera-Band" to stretch around my foot and allow me to do an exercise where I point my toes as if I was a ballerina. The Thera-Band then pulls the foot back up. Those are the muscles that I lost. I did three sets of twenty-five of these yesterday and really pushed in the hope of developing the unused pushing muscles. Apparently, I did a little too much as the leg swelled up a little and split the wound open at the edge of the eschara. There was a bleeding to go along with the swelling and puffy, sore skin this morning. Vicodin is good!

We made a call to the visiting nurse "hotline" to see if we needed to go to the emergency room. After a discussion, we realized it was the exercise that hastened the eschara splitting off from the good tissue. The nurse was pleased that there was blood and not smelly puss. The eschara has to come off, and either my body will do it as it is now, or a doctor has to remove it with a blade. I am scheduled for a wound center visit and expect that they will finish removing what my body has already begun to remove.

Dealing with this radiated tissue is turning out to be more involved than I first thought. The tissue does not respond to care like the rest of my leg. The original incision was about sixteen to eighteen inches long. The top four inches and the bottom three inches are completely healed with the typical railroad-track scar. The middle ten inches or so is a mess of leathery eschara tissue that has to come off one way or the other.

Anyone out there have experience with this sort of thing? Any suggestions? I am about ready to open up my penknife and start carving this stuff off.

WRITTEN AUGUST 4, 2010, 9:38 A.M.

Things seemed to have slowed down. Weekly visits to the surgeon with little change that I see, but people seem to be pleased with how it is going. I guess I wasn't supposed to be vertical and on a cane so early. The real bottom line is that I am chomping at the bit to do things and I just can't do them now. The worst part is thinking that I may never be able to do them again.

Yesterday, I was measured for my "AFO." It's a foot-drop brace, and I don't know why they just didn't call it a "FDB." The thing is made of space-age plastic and comes up to mid-calf area and then down under my foot. It holds my foot up so that I can swing my leg more naturally as I walk. Right now, in order to walk, I have to lean way over to the right to pull my leg up far enough for my dragging toes not to hit the floor. I now have a sore back as a result. The AFO does help a lot, and my brace should be in by Friday or next Monday at the latest. I had to buy "deep" shoes made especially for these braces. I can't believe we had to spend $125.00 for shoes that Frankenstein would wear. All I need are two electrodes on the neck, and I am ready for Halloween. I am disgusted with that.

The doctor told me that next week he may start cutting down the eschara to allow my healing to continue. My guess is maybe November 1st before the wound is closed completely. That radiation did a real number on me. The part of the leg that was not radiated has been healed completely for three weeks already.

WRITTEN AUGUST 5, 2010, 7:36 P.M.

Heard back from my dermatologist today, and the biopsy he did on my nose came back as cancer. I have a basal cell carcinoma and must have it removed. I have been referred to a doctor who specializes in "Mohs surgery." I am going for a consultation on August 19th.

This medical stuff is getting kind of old. By the way, thank you, Judy, for taking me "behind the woodshed" a bit. Your truth and personal experience were just what I needed today.

WRITTEN AUGUST 6, 2010, 8:43 P.M.

Thank you, Pastor Andy, and his wife, Laura, for your visit this evening after the conference you both were attending. I am jealous of your stamina. Thank you also for the book *The Land Between* by Jeff Manion. I have started it.

Perhaps a little explanation is in order here. Pastor Andy read a tweet of mine that conveyed pretty clearly that I was a little down concerning my physical trials (i.e., new cancer on the nose, slow healing of my leg, etc.). I always appreciate his council and a visit from Laura. Andy was moved to bring me the book tonight because he heard the author, Jeff Manion, speaking today and felt that I needed to read what Jeff had to say. Manion uses the biblical story of the Israelites journey through the Sinai Desert as a metaphor for being in an undesired transitional place.

The book *The Land Between* was written for people who are experiencing:

> » Fear of an uncertain future

> » Unemployment

> » Foreclosure

> » Illness

> » Family crisis

I have only just begun the book but was so taken by the opening prayer that I felt that I had to share it with you, as it is the perfect prayer for me to pray about my illnesses. I hope you are moved by it as well. He calls it "My prayer for you":

My prayer for you as you read this book is that God will visit you with Grace in your season of transition. I pray that the barren landscape of trial will become the fertile soil for new growth. May our gracious God revive your spirit and restore your laughter. May you find Him in your pain and trust Him in your waiting. May the One who redeems all things meet you powerfully as you journey through the Land Between.

Thank you, Andy. I am sure the book will be a great read.

WRITTEN AUGUST 9, 2010, 8:46 P.M.

I am trying to listen to the doctors and visiting nurses and slow down. I guess I have been pushing it a bit and got myself into a little trouble with swelling and pain. I exercised, but too much. Go figure.

The Connecticut primaries are tomorrow, and Cindy is putting in a sixteen-hour day in place of me. I am bummed about that, but what a trooper she is. I definitely married "up" with her.

I finished the book that Pastor Andy gave me in time to return it to him on Sunday. It had a very appropriate message for me and for anyone else concerned about a life crisis. It was a good read for me at this time. I had wandered from my core beliefs and needed to get back into familiar territory.

Our summer here in Connecticut has been the best that I can remember. Our electric bill at $289 reflects the amount of AC that we used, but boy was it ever worth it. Boston is only four games out of the wildcard, so life is good. I should be hearing about my final brace this week, so hopefully, I can begin practice walking with it. I have not been down to the big boat at all this summer, so I am looking forward to a visit before school starts.

WRITTEN AUGUST 12, 2010, 6:39 P.M.

(This entry is not for the weak of stomach, especially before a meal,)

Well, today has been an interesting day. Once per week, I have been returning to the surgeon who operated on me for his wound follow-up. I believe that I mentioned to you that a hard scab called eschara had formed where my leg had been radiated. Well, today's short version is that that eschara was cut off this morning and that the underlying wound was scraped until fresh blood was present on all tissue, and then a "wound vacuum pump" was installed. This pump forces the body to continuously bathe the open tissue with body fluids to promote very fast healing. Leaving the eschara might result in a healed wound in six months, but the pump should do it in one month.

Unfortunately, I am kind of grossed out by the whole process and my stomach has been turning over all day. I have to carry around a four-pound pump with tubing connected to a drain in my leg for a month, and it must be 24-7.

On the bright side, my surgeon was thrilled with the fact that I walked into his office today. I found out that he did not expect me to be on my feet for several months yet. I have been pushing myself, and apparently, that was a good thing.

So in summary, I am healing beautifully per the surgeon and all the visiting nurses, yet I am grossed out by the methodology used to affect the healing.

It seems that God does have a sense of humor, and He is laughing at me now. All I can say is this: "Okay, God, what's next?"

WRITTEN AUGUST 15, 2010, 11:35 P.M.

I have gotten used to the wound pump, and it no longer grosses me out. I was able to purchase a covering for the tubing so no one has to see the lymph flowing through. All that is seen is my "man bag" slung over my shoulder and a black cloth pipe connected to me.

At first, the pump produced a mild burning sensation, but now I feel nothing. The area around the wound is warm to the touch and red. The pump is at work in this tissue.

My walking has gotten more labored with the pump attached, so I am back in the wheelchair. Several people in the church were curious as to why I use a wheelchair now but walked last week. The wound pump is the reason. I absolutely did not suffer a setback. In fact, the wound pump is a good thing and was planned by the surgeon ever since my operation. Taking off the eschara was not pleasant, and walking is somewhat more difficult again; however, the benefit of the faster healing via the pump will be well worth it.

I was unable to get my final leg brace fitted because the open wound prevents my strapping it on over my calf. It will have to wait.

I will be working on some light foot exercising so that I don't allow it to take a permanent drop position.

Life is good. I don't know why I have been so blessed with the successful operation and recovery from this extensive surgery. I continue to be amazed by the photographs the doctor gave me of the actual operation and the removed cancer. If I have a family member who would like to see them, please contact me.

WRITTEN AUGUST 21, 2010, 6:54 A.M.

Just a short entry to let you know what's up. I have been on the wound pump for one week now, and the "newness" has worn off. It is a bit of a pain to haul around with me 24-7. It looks like I am wearing a "man purse" with tubes running into my pants! I do get looks when I am out. The thing has a life of its own, gurgling and grunting from time to time and usually at the wrong time like in church or in a checkout line. It maintains a partial vacuum on the wound and encourages the body to provide refreshing nutrients to the site so much needed skin can grow. For the most part, the wound itself is healed, but there is no skin covering at this point. The deepest part of the wound is maybe three eighths of an inch, but it is two inches wide. The bottom of the wound is nice and pink now and bleeds readily when the doctor scraps "slough" away. They tell me that this is very good.

I am looking forward to fitting the final brace on my leg but must wait a bit longer for the healing process to nearly complete. I walk very unsteadily and hope that the brace will make a big difference. I am less conscious of my Frankenstein shoes as they are at least comfortable. Cindy has been great, and as a matter of fact, it is our twenty-ninth anniversary today. Who would have thought that she could endure that long? It must be the Schulte magnetism that does it.

What a summer we have had. The weather has been unbelievably beautiful and hot. I thank God that our home has central air. The electric company has sent us a letter of thanks along with our biggest bills ever. I hope that all of you have enjoyed the heat one way or another. It will be back to school in just a couple of weeks here. My boat never left the garage, but I have great hopes of spending meaningful time in it next year. The worst part of this whole deal has been the fact that I have not been on the water. I plan to take a ride or two on M/V Becky Thatcher before she closes, but I'd better heal fast as the season is slowly coming to a close. Summer hours end with August, and she will not run every day after that.

WRITTEN AUGUST 27, 2010, 9:37 P.M.

My last entry was a week ago, and there has not been a whole lot of exciting things going on. I continue to see the surgeon weekly, and he says I will be seeing him for some time to come. He is beginning to be optimistic about my healing, perhaps without a future skin graft, which I do not want if at all possible. I continue to use a wound pump, and it is an amazing device. My visiting nurses marvel at the changes they see.

I was measured for my AFO brace a couple of weeks back, and today, I was fitted for it. At first, I thought that I would be able to get used to its tight fit, but within two hours of leaving Surgi-Care, the provider, I was back on the phone with them because it was just too tight and beginning to chaff badly. I will be back in there on Monday afternoon, and they say that they have many ways to change the fit of the brace and trim pinch points if necessary. I trust them as they have a great reputation, and I probably should not have left there with the tight fit. They also provided me with a sleeping brace. One of the problems for folks with drop foot is that scar tissue can form overnight if a sleeping brace is not worn, and it can accumulate to the point where the AFO day braces can no longer hold the foot up without considerable pain. The night brace is actually more comfortable than sleeping without one as the foot is more moveable in the morning and it is easier to get started walking each morning. Without the brace, I have had a couple of mornings when I just had to stand next to the bed, rocking back and forth to get the ankle joint moving again.

I continue to be impressed with the quality of care I am getting from my providers. Having said that, I am blown out of the water with how expensive it is. My AFO brace, which is made in Sweden (thank God not China), is made of carbon fiber and extremely lightweight, perhaps one pound. It is over $900.00, and the sleep brace is another $250.00. My insurance covered it all. So far, my costs for all of my care have been the cost of gasoline going back and forth to providers and hospitals.

My thanks go out again to all of you well-wishers. I appreciate all the support that I have received.

WRITTEN SEP. 3, 2010, 3:08 P.M.

Well, it has been yet another week of playing the waiting game with my leg. I continue to use the wound pump to good advantage. Two thirds of my wound has "super granulated" (That means that the hamburger has risen over the level of surrounding skin, which means that we will not use the pump on two thirds of the wound.) Those two thirds will be covered with something called zero-form gauze (Vaseline-impregnated gauze), which will keep the surface from forming a scab and allow the skin along the edges to slowly encroach on the wound and eventually heal it completely. The bottom third of the wound still is about three eights of an inch deep by three inches long and two inches wide. The wound pump has been adjusted to fit snuggly around that area. I expect about two more weeks on the pump.

My foot brace has been modified, and it is no longer so tight that it chaffs. It is still not comfortable, but at least it does not hurt. I can wear it for several hours before I have to take it off. Tomorrow will be a big test for it as I plan, weather permitting, to ride on M/V Becky Thatcher and catch up with friends.

My doctors seem pleased with my recovery (which I think is dead slow). I wore my brace into the surgeon's office, and he was pleased to see me without a cane. I can walk okay without a cane, but not too far. I still need it. I will be happy when I no longer need it as I have developed a decidedly back-and-forth-swaying limp when I use it, and it is going to be a tough habit to break. When someone has a condition like mine, they tend to lean forward and stare down at the ground in order to pick out a safe place to step. When I stand erect now, it feels strange indeed.

Being as limited as I am, I now celebrate the smaller things: a hot cup of coffee, sitting out on the deck, a good game of cards (win or lose), an ice cream sundae.

All of these things have lifted my spirits when I have been down a bit. I saw an interesting video on YouTube that I suggest you watch. It's only a couple of minutes long. Go to youtube.com and search for "no arms, no legs, no worries." It was a kick in the pants that I needed at the time, and God just placed it there for me.

I am off now to Rich's birthday party (son-in-law). I hope the pizza is nice and hot.

As always, you guys have treated me better than I deserve. I am blessed to have you as friends. Stay well!

WRITTEN SEP. 6, 2010, 7:48 P.M.

I need to write a short update for the folks who still follow this blog. (I know I have used the word short before and then run on a bit, but not this time.)

First, my brace is working out fine. I am walking longer on it each day.

Second, my wound pump failed yesterday because we asked it to do something it cannot, and the visiting nurses had to send out a problem-solver to make things right. All okay now.

Third and most importantly, when I was in the rehab facility under the influence of various opiates, someone gave me a book to read when I got a chance. The book is titled *Captured by Grace* by the Rev. David Jeremiah. I have just now started the book and am halfway through it and very impressed and touched by its content. I apologize for not remembering who gave it to me, and I would like to chat with you about this book. My recording secretary, Cindy, doesn't know either. Please forgive me, but please tell me if you gave me that book.

Thank you in advance.

WRITTEN SEP. 6, 2010, 11:51 P.M.

See what happens when I try to be brief? I miss items of interest to folks.

Cindy and I did get to have our riverboat ride on Saturday. The wind was not a problem, as it was only blowing ten knots from up river. The return trip from the bridge was excellent. We almost did not get to go as two Bobs showed up and they said they were looking for stowaways. I appreciate the welcome we received by the entire crew and management team. I even got a hug from the track superintendent. I was shaky by the time we got home as it was my first outing without the wheelchair. It was great! I will be visiting the office in a couple of weeks.

Bruce was interested in the wound pump, and we had our first failure this weekend. The VNA had to dispatch one of their best on Saturday to remedy the problem. Bottom line was that the Vaseline in the zero-form gauze liquefied when combined with normal body fluids and began to loosen the Tegaderm adhesive bandage. She got to me before it actually leaked, but it would have been a mess. The method we used was an attempt to treat a third of the wound with vacuum and the rest with the moist zero-form. This is cutting-edge stuff, and we have found out that we have to use another method to isolate parts of the wound. I will give you all the gory details when the new bandage design is actually in place. The wound itself is down to about ten inches long by an inch and a half wide at it widest point. It is only about three eighths of an inch deep now in the deepest one-third area. It is going to leave a dandy divot scar, but I don't really care. They had to use about fifty square inches of cadaver skin to put things back together inside my leg, and my body is now breaking down that material after it did the job of holding various parts of me in place for the large external wound to heal. The large volume of liquids being pulled out of the wound includes this breakdown of cadaver skin. Based on this operation, I am going to donate more of me to science after I die. I can only thank my cadaver donor for some of his body parts.

I keep finding out more about this operation as I visit the doctor weekly. I am blown away by the amount of reconstruction he had to do. No wonder it took him eight hours to do it. I have found out that five doctors were involved at various times supporting my surgeon.

I have no feeling on the left side of my leg below the knee or on top of my foot or toes. Oddly, I can feel my ankle all around. I can point my foot but cannot retract it, so I use the AFO brace to bring it back to perpendicular with my leg. The brace also gives me a springy step to match my good leg. The brace is made completely out of carbon fiber, weighs about ten ounces, and costs over $900.00. By the way, it was made in Sweden, at least not in China.

Walking with the brace still feels strange, but I do not limp with the brace unless I am tired. The doctor wants me to start walking and increase the distance each day. I can walk about a hundred feet without much of a limp at this point. I still have to climb stairs one at a time and lead with my good foot. I have to sit down to put my pants on, as balancing right now is out of the question. When I stand, I need to hesitate and get my balance squared away before I walk. All of these things have gotten better slowly, and I anticipate near normalcy when this thing is done healing.

I see the light at the end of the tunnel, and it is not a train. I am, however, focusing on the "now" and have a few places I want to visit in the not-too-distant future. Cindy and I are headed to California in December to visit my oldest friend of over sixty years. I think I met Paul when I was about four years old, and we have been in touch ever since. I will be adding pictures soon and will let you know when I have uploaded them. The pictures of the operation itself will not be uploaded as they are rather graphic. If anyone is truly interested in seeing them, you will just have to visit me.

WRITTEN SEP. 12, 2010, 12:41 A.M.

Well, the wound pump is off ... at least for the time being. My surgeon wants to give me a week healing on my own, and we will see if I still know how to grow skin. Wish me luck or more preferably, say a prayer for a good outcome. I don't want to deal with skin grafts if I don't have to.

Cindy is bandaging my leg now, the visiting nurses coming just three times per week. We are using a wet-to-dry bandage in the deepest area and Telfa on the rest. I get to take long showers with this bandage. With the wound pump, it was all sponge baths, which I hate now.

WRITTEN SEP. 14, 2010, 5:16 P.M.

This journal entry is a "Can you top this week?" challenge.

1. On Monday, I had a doctor's appointment with my primary care physician. This is a normal six-month short visit to confirm that blood pressure, heart rhythm, and everything else is okay.

2. On Tuesday, I had my first meeting and evaluation with my respiratory doctor, who is running my sleep disorder therapy.

3. On Thursday afternoon, I have my regular weekly meeting with my surgeon for follow-up on the wound, which is healing slowly from the cancer operation in June.

4. On Thursday evening, I will be overnighting at the sleep disorder center in West Hartford. Two technicians will be evaluating my sleep habits. It should be noted that the respiratory doctor sent me home from the hospital after the operation with a cutting-edge CPAP machine that has been recording my sleep traits. Even with the CPAP machine, I stopped breathing as many as sixteen times per hour. I get out of the sleep test at 7:00 a.m. Friday morning. Just in time for—

5. At 7:30 on Friday morning, I report to a clinic in Wethersfield for my Mohs surgery. This surgery will remove a basal cell carcinoma where my nose and cheek meet.

If you think you can top this week of doctor's visits, evaluations, and surgery, please leave a message in the guestbook, and we can get together for a lunch sometime. Of course, any comment is welcome.

Update: *Oh, and I forgot, tucked in between these appointments are three visits from the visiting nurses who keep their professional eye on my leg, bandage, and make recommendations to the surgeon for follow-up care.*

WRITTEN SEP. 18, 2010, 8:42 P.M.

Whew ... I am glad that week is over. It felt like we lived in waiting rooms. The most memorable events of the week were the overnight sleep study and the removal of the basal cell carcinoma. I overnighted in the sleep lab on Thursday night, and while I do not have the official report back, I know I have sleep apnea as the technician fitted me with a CPAP machine at about 12:30 a.m. in order to study the results when she adjusted the air pressures on the CPAP remotely. I was wired up with about twenty wires all over my head and body. I was surprised to see that they cemented the pads to me and then removed the cemented pads with acetone the next morning. My hair was a mess and matted down as if I hadn't washed it in a month. I rushed home to shower so that I could be at the dermatologist's by 7:30 a.m.

The operation to remove the basal cell cancer was anything but easy. He explained that the numbing needles would be painful as they had to use a chemical that would not discolor the skin like most other Novocain-type drugs. I had to take four initial shots in the nose and cheek and seven more shots after the numbing solution started to take hold. The first four shots were very painful, and tears were streaming down my face, which I was told was normal being that the shots were so close to the eyes and nose. The operation took about an hour and a half, and he had to go back in and cut some more after the initial biopsy showed cancer cells along the edges. He used five internal stitches to partially close the wound and eleven more on the surface of the skin to finish the job. It sounds worse than it looks as the stitches are all in the crease between my nose and cheek. I don't think there will be much of a scar. The bandage he put on is called a pressure bandage, and it is thick and stiff, about the same size as my nose so I look like something off of a UFO. I am back on Vicodin for the pain and not allowed to blow my nose, sneeze, puff up my cheeks, lift anything heavy, or get angry at someone (red-faced anger). Friday was not comfortable; however, by Saturday, the pain was under control, and now I am just resting until Monday when I am supposed to remove the bandage and go to Band-Aids.

As I mentioned in my Facebook page: "Missing church tomorrow because of the pressure bandage and stitches in my face. I have the Frankenstein walk down pat. I have his shoes. Now I am working on the scars on the face. Do you think sixteen stitches is enough? I still need electrodes for my neck and a sparking power source. I hope to be done for Halloween."

WRITTEN SEP. 21, 2010, 11:13 P.M.

A special request. Tonight, I received word that my older brother, Joe, is in the ICU of a hospital in New Jersey. Many of you have been so supportive of me and my battle with cancer. Your prayers have worked miracles with my health, and I am asking that you raise up my brother Joe and his wife, Joan, during this serious illness. Thank you for being here for me.

Bob

WRITTEN OCTOBER 1, 2010, 9:25 P.M.

This is the longest time between updates. Things are definitely slowing down from my perspective, and I am trying to decide whether to continue with updates or just suspend things for a while; however, here are some items to report.

Thank you for all those who offered well-wishes and prayers for my brother Joe. He is now in an acute care rehab facility in New Jersey, and it will be some time before we know what his long-term prognosis will be. Please keep him on your prayer lists.

The surgery on my nose went painfully well, and now that the stitches are out, it is hard to find the scar. The doctor skillfully placed them right in the crease that is formed where my nose meets my cheek. If I ever have that type of surgery again, it will be under a more general anesthesia.

The progress on my leg has been measurable on a weekly basis for the past several months, but now it has slowed to barely discernible. I can wear the brace for about six hours before the leg starts to tighten up and the Vicodin vial comes out. I can walk probably three hundred yards and then must sit and go into a people-watching mode, not so bad if you are in a high-traffic area like an airport, not so good anywhere in Durham. I need to work on balance, balance, balance. I never realized how much one needs both legs for balance. I tip over to the right if I don't wear the brace, and standing up in the dark is exciting.

I have always said that miracles result from earnest prayer, but I did not think that I would ever be so close to one. It has been a real roller-coaster ride for the past nine months, which begs the question, "What would I ever have done without my best friend, Jesus Christ?"

I had my first three-month CAT scan last week, and my lungs are clear. (The cancer that I once had can attack the lungs after doing its thing in the limbs.)

Cindy has survived her bout with shingles and her allergy to the meds. She has not taken a painkiller for two days, and her spirits lifted after taking prednisone for six days. It was rough there for a while. I thought I might have to get up and take care of myself, but she worked right through it. LOL. It must be her Maine stock.

We are both getting over killer colds and starting to brace for the busy work involved in setting up the November election in Durham. I am registrar, and Cindy is deputy registrar of voters. We both enjoy the work very much.

Finally, I want to tell you that I am discussing opportunities to be of some use to the Essex Steam Train and Riverboat Organization (Valley Railroad). That group has been so great. I only hope that I can return the favor in some way. I love being able to say that my train set weighs around two hundred tons and is "one-to-one scale."

WRITTEN OCTOBER 29, 2010, 10:03 P.M.

Recently, I have received several nice notes from friends of mine who want to see at least occasional updates. I owe that to anyone who has followed my wordy journal for all these months. Here is a quick (less than two page) heads-up on what has been going on.

I am right now approaching the finish line for the 2010 midterm election (I am registrar of voters here in Durham), so one reason I have not written is that I have been busy ... or maybe struggling to keep up is the best way to describe it. The other day, I really tested myself and my endurance when I was bringing voting machines and supplies over to the polling place. It was only a couple of hundred pounds in six or seven pieces, but you would have thought they were a ton each by the way I handled them. I am not taking that to mean I will always struggle with that kind of carrying. I believe I will get stronger than I am now, but I need to be careful.

I have asked my doctors for and received scripts for physical therapy. I am unsure enough on my feet to know that falling down is not a maybe thing, but it's more a when thing. I have had four good sessions so far, and I am learning wonderful exercises for balance control. I am going to Middlesex Hospital's Rehabilitation Clinic, and the machines they have there are great. My favorite incorporates a video game full of mazes you have to navigate by tilting a dish that you stand on in all different directions. There are two railings to hold on to, but they try to get you to use first two hands, then one hand, then two fingers, and then nothing while you are navigating through the mazes. They also have a bull's-eye target that you struggle to maintain a light point in center. When I was evaluated on this machine, I scored very poorly. I look forward to getting my feet under me and working on the score. The full range of the measurement was from zero (best) to five (extremely poor), and I scored a 5.4, which falls off the scale.

I am also having another biopsy done, this time on my ear. I see a dermatologist every ninety days, and he found what may be a basal cell carcinoma on the top of my ear, which I have burned in the sun while I have been sailing at least a gazillion times. It is not a big deal.

My leg wound is now being allowed to scab up as they no longer want to keep it open. The inner tissue has grown almost to the surface of my leg, and the divot, the deepest part, is almost filled.

Visiting nurses no longer visit me because I was released from their care this past Wednesday. They were great and very reassuring for Cindy as she was dressing my wound four or five days per week when the nurses were not visiting on a daily basis. It was good to have professional eyes on the wound a couple of times per week. Sometimes it looked kind of scary, but the nurses loved raw meat and running blood in the wound. They claimed the blood carried the needed nutrients to the burned area (radiation burns).

I have gotten to the point when I can wear my brace twelve hours or longer if absolutely necessary. I can also wear tall leather boots like my motorcycle boots and get enough support from the stiff leather uppers. My cowboy boots do not have enough support. Such is life.

I took time to read some of my older postings. Some I liked. Some I didn't. But that was where I was at the time, so I will leave them as I wrote them. A couple of them reminded me of some of the hurdles that we jumped together. Your support, visits, phone calls, and notes were amazing. I wish that I could repay your kindness in some way. I hope to do so by passing it on to needy nursing home residents in our area. I have not been able to do much of that yet, but I promised myself that after election, I would make a real effort. If any of you would like to come along, please write or call.

Well, I will go for now. My prayer for you tonight is that you enjoy your family as I enjoy mine and that day by day, they come closer to our Lord Jesus Christ.

WRITTEN NOVEMBER 27, 2010, 6:28 P.M.

Here is an update on what is happening around here.

My leg is almost healed. I would guess another month, and the lesion will be closed completely. I wear a Telfa bandage on the wound to keep it from scabbing over and to allow the skin to heal from the sides. It is working.

The physical training is great, but it takes its toll on me. I no longer have a complete fibula bone. About three inches after it leaves the ankle it has been removed up to the knee. In addition to the bone, the doctor removed three muscles, including the soleus and the tibialis anterior. Then he moved another by rolling it over to fill the void created by the removals. As a result, I am learning new things about my leg weekly. I no longer have a classic anatomy, and the PT therapists marvel at what I am able to do with what "I got." The downside is that there is an absolute end to how good I will ever be without those muscles and bone, not to mention the peroneal nerve, which is no longer there either. I have to be careful to not expect my leg to act normal. I had a little excitement last night as we went to the emergency room to have my leg checked out. It had swollen badly over the stump of the fibula, coming out of the ankle, and it was a nasty red in color with sensitivity to the surface of the skin. I honestly could not tell if I had cellulitis, some sort of abrasion on the skin, or as the doctor warned, a bone infection. The result was four X-rays that confirmed that the bone was fine and the likely culprit was four days of unusual activity combined with two especially tough PT sessions. The moral of the story is that I now have different limits on my activities than I had before, and I have to be aware of them.

My brace, which I had been able to wear for up to twelve hours, is no longer comfortable after about four hours, and it won't be until the swelling goes down.

Having said all of the above, what I am presented with is a healthy changed leg that has limitations that I need to manage. Some days, I will be wearing a brace only, and my gait will be semi-normal. On other days, I will be limping a bit and using a cane so I don't have to wear the brace as much. The limp does not represent a setback at all but rather a break from the brace.

Cindy and I are grateful for our situation right now. I am currently cancer-free and don't dwell on the prospects of it coming back. We are enjoying our friends and grandchildren, and we love to visit and have visitors. We are headed off to California on Tuesday to visit my oldest friend. Paulie and I go back to 1949 or 1950 when we discovered each other living on the same block in Bloomfield, NJ. So it is a friendship of over sixty years. Paul is a success story in two careers. He was a sought-after computer programmer during the heyday, and he purchased various California properties thirty years ago. After he retired (early), he went on to produce Hawaiian slack key guitar CDs. So far, he has won four Grammy awards.

During the next few weeks, we will be working up to Christmas, which is a very important event for our family. God has been very near me during 2010, so I can't say that I am glad the year will be over soon. I sit here more in a state of awe that He chose to honor so many of my friends' prayers. I find myself speechless to be able to describe the wonder.

May God bless you and your families during this season. May He keep you safe and bring you home from your travels, and may you get to know Him better and better with each passing day.

Thank you for being my friends.

WRITTEN MARCH 1, 2011, 9:57 P.M.

It has been a while since I journalled. Life is great, and the changes that Cindy and I are going through are fascinating. My illness really thrust me fully into retirement. I left two of my jobs and income sources behind because captaining boats and carrying computers around is pretty much out of the question for me. Late last, fall I piloted M/V Becky Thatcher for a while as I was visiting for the day, but it was clear that I could not function as a captain should. I would be ill-equipped to assist in a man-overboard or shipboard fire. I would be an added risk to the passengers. Strangely, I was not upset about it. I look at it as a necessary corner that I have turned in a wonderful life.

The whole walking thing has gotten my attention. I am functioning at a rather low level of endurance. My concern is not for now but rather for how I will be doing in ten years. Of course, that ten years is not guaranteed for any of us and certainly not for someone who has had three different types of cancer, counting the basal cell carcinomas I have recently had removed from my nose and right ear.

I feel really well and do not believe that I have an active cancer somewhere else in my body. I am nervous a bit about a comprehensive scan that I will be getting done on March 17th and would appreciate your prayers for a clean bill of health. I think this scan is a combination of two contrasting MRIs and a CAT scan all combined in a computer to build a 3-D model of yours truly. Pretty space-age stuff.

I hope that all of you survived the snow okay. This was a most vexing winter for both Cindy and me as we really tried to avoid walking on any ice or snow. As a result, we had cabin fever on several occasions. Our church and friends have been great, and we continue to try to not overuse our friendships. I do want to say, however, that the help we have been given moving heavier objects, climbing up a ladder, or shoveling a path to the street is greatly appreciated.

Well, that's it for now. I will be back to you after the 17th.

Chapter 6

LEANING ON HIM

Eight-thirty p.m., and I'm trying to absorb everything that happened today. Bottom line is that the doctors have found a mass in my right lung that is consistent with the cancer that I had in my leg. My leg seems to be clear. The leg cancer called "fibrous histiocytoma" is a sarcoma that spreads hemotropically (through the blood). There is no way to tell if the mass is actually the same cancer. It was not there three months ago in a CAT scan, and it is plainly visible now. It must come out as soon as possible, and I am visiting a cardiothoracic surgeon on next Monday. I could be back in surgery within a couple of weeks. It is a small mass about the size of your pinky fingernail (1.3cm). My leg surgeon could not predict whether it could be operated on laparoscopically (go in from under the rib cage) or if they would have to open the chest. My mind is running pretty fast right now, and I am glad that I have Jesus and Cindy to lean on heavily.

Robert R. Schulte

Written March 22, 2011, 5:20 p.m.

Here is the latest information: Cindy and I spent four hours at St. Francis Hospital yesterday, meeting with our new cardiothoracic surgeon, Dr. T. He is a personable guy, and he spent all the time we wanted discussing my situation. He believes that I have a "metastasized" cancer from my leg, but he reiterated that we would not know absolutely until after an operation and subsequent biopsy. He described the operation in detail for us. It will be accomplished through three small openings between my ribs, two under my right arm and one through my back. He will deflate the right lung by going down my throat with a tool that will inflate a small balloon, blocking air from my right lung. He will manipulate the lung after it is deflated through one hole, view it through a scope in another hole, and cut and resection it through the last hole. The operation should take two hours, and I will be in the hospital for two or three days. Recovery will be at home with a plethora of drugs.

It is interesting how the mind can handle these things if there is an understanding of what is going to happen. I think I am getting used to the idea that I have a serious cancer. I plan to spend quality time on more pithy activities with family, friends, and church.

The operation is scheduled for next Wednesday, March 30th. I told them I wanted to get it over with so I could spend quality time sitting around the pool next summer, something I totally missed because of my June surgery last year.

Written March 28, 2011, 3:03 p.m.

In forty-eight hours, I will be checking into St. Francis Hospital for the next round of cancer surgery. Before I go further, I want to write about the tremendous support that I have received from my family and friends. It is both very humbling and gratifying to experience the prayers, affection, and well-wishes from so many people who are important to me. Thank you very much!

So on Wednesday, it begins again. I am definitely not looking forward to the operation, but it is the only thing I can do. At this point, they (the doctors) can not guarantee that the spot on my lung is the same cancer as my leg, but it is very probable (80 percent) that it is. As I mentioned before, the type of cancer I had in my leg can travel through the bloodstream.

My senses at this point are pretty dull. I avoid thinking about it by doing other things that I like, such as working on the computer, playing my new ukulele, or watching basketball on TV. The NCAA tournament has been a blessing to me this year.

Strangely, I don't feel ill. The spot on the lung is so small that I have no shortness of breath, and if I wanted too complain, the only thing I could say was that my leg is very stiff and tight from all of the scar tissue.

(Phone call.)

That was the hospital. I now have to be in St. Francis at 6:00 a.m. on Wednesday as I will be first in line for the operating table. The operating room last time was absolutely freezing. When I commented on that, I was told that the cold keeps germs at bay while in the operating room. I guess I am glad that they take that precaution as I don't want to pick up some superbug while I am in there.

Mentally, I am doing well. When I was born, my folks did not receive a warranty on me for X number of years. None of you have that warranty either. Now I am blessed by God because I am being forced to at least consider my mortality and my immortality after my stay on this earth. So many people drop dead or are killed in accidents, and they never have the opportunity to get their house in order. I do have that opportunity, and I am trying to clean up loose ends. My whole life has been an E ticket ride with God providing adventure, safety, blessings of comfortable living, and absolutely wonderful friends. With His help, my life has been a success. I fall so far short of being a "good Christian."

I am embarrassed sometimes when I go to God with my requests. So many others suffer so horribly in poverty and dangerous conditions around the world that I question whether I have the right to go to the Father for assistance. It is through my Bible reading, however, that it becomes apparent that God wants us to rely on Him. So here I am, God, asking for and expecting a miracle. I'll check back with You tonight. Meanwhile, thank You for my friends and family and especially for Cindy, who has been my constant companion for these thirty years.

WRITTEN MARCH 30, 2011, 7:00 P.M. BY CINDY SCHULTE

Hello, friends and family,

Thank you so much for all your prayers. Bob went through surgery with flying colors! The doctor said he got the cancer (it was) but sees no more, and Bob got through it very nicely. Saw him after and was amazed at how alert he was. (Something about having an epidural, I am sure.) Dr. T said he will just need to check every three months to make sure no more comes back, but for now, Bob is clean.

I know all of your prayers got all of us through this day today, and I can't thank you enough. When Bob is back on to report, he will be happy to fill you in on the details. He asked for malted milk balls tomorrow. Praise God! It was a good day.

Cindy

WRITTEN MARCH 31, 2011, 9:47 P.M. BY CINDY SCHULTE

It's Cindy again, but this will be the last day. Bob is coming home tomorrow. I am picking him up before 11:00 a.m. Spent the afternoon with him, and he is ready to come home. I'll let him fill you in, but we'll be home by mid-early afternoon, watching the snow (or rain) on April 1st.

We are blessed to have such friends. Feel free to call or stop by.

WRITTEN APRIL 1, 2011, 2:11 P.M.

Just a quick note: I am home, exhausted because you don't sleep in hospitals. I have much to tell, but I am too sore to sit here and type. The epidural (nerve block) between my shoulders did wonders for me for the first day and a half after the surgery. Now that it has worn off, I am on the narcotics, oxycodone, and two Percocets. The first is a twelve-hour baseline pain reliever, and the two Percocets are bombs for breakthrough pain. I almost want the pain. The Percocets make me loonier than Charlie Sheen.

WRITTEN APRIL 2, 2011, 9:26 A.M.

On Wednesday morning, we had to be at the admitting office early. Traffic at 5:30 a.m. was moderate even at that early hour. Cindy and I were limping into the hospital, and immediately, we were offered a ride on an electric cart. Vicki was providing us with morale support, so she was able to ride along with us.

There was a registration process in an office and then a short wait for an admitting bed to be assigned. All of the paperwork had to be put in order. They even had to mark my body with magic marker to identify which side was to be operated on. It was here that we met with the surgeon, Dr. T, and two anesthesiologists who provided us with information on forms indicating the extent of the operation and the anesthesia, which was planned. The anesthesiologist was really selling us on his epidural process because of the anticipated recovery pain. He made his case, so we okayed that. I had to sign off on the forms—a nice touch. IVs were inserted, blood type taken yet again, and PT-INR testing done pre-op as I take Coumadin (a blood thinner) for atrial fibrillation.

We were visited by St. Francis's chaplain, who offered prayer and a blessing. It was a nice touch. Earlier in the week, Pastor Andy and the entire church staff surrounded me in the church office, and we had prayer as well. You might say that my operation was bathed in prayer, and believe you me, it made a huge difference to me, knowing that God was invited to the party.

All of this took about one busy hour. By this time, I had to "go" and was in my new garb, the hated "Johnny." Luckily, the bathroom was right across the hall, so I was able to be discreet.

All was now in readiness, so Vicki, Cindy, and I had prayer and said our good-byes. They wheeled me off to the operating room. The room seemed smallish to me at sixteen by sixteen feet. On TV, the rooms seem so much larger. It was filled with lots of stainless steel racks upon which hundreds of scissors, clamps, and bandages were all stacked neatly for the day. That same sight unnerved me a bit during my last operation.

Epidural anesthesia (nerve block) is given through the lower back to many moms in the delivery room. My epidural was given to me between my shoulder blades. I was asked to sit on the operating table on a thick pad and bend way forward into a large pillow that I clutched to my chest. I had to hunch up my back while I buried my face in the pillow. A nurse then stood in front of me and gave me a nice big hug. (That was the last thing I remember.). She apparently was there to prevent me from falling off the table when the catheter went in. The operation lasted about two hours, and I woke up refreshed and in "zero" pain in the recovery room at 10:55.

The doctor called Cindy at 10:30 and told her about the operation and that all had gone well. He was able to close off my right lung as planned using the suction/balloon device that went down my throat. Then three incisions were made between different ribs. Two cuts were right under my right arm and one in my back on the right side. A video camera went in one, and a manipulating tool and a cutting tool went in the other two. The collapsed right lung was like a limp balloon, and they were able to turn it all around to see the outside surfaces. Dr. T could not see the cancer as it was in the wall of the lung. He had to manipulate it until he could feel the mass with his finger. The mass was "excised" and sent to pathology for evaluation.

Pathology was involved to (1) determine that it was a cancerous growth (and it was) and (2) make sure that there were no cancerous cells along the cut edges (and there were none).

The pain is caused by the damage done to the ribs when they are pried apart to reach inside. They use a special anesthetic that lasts the first twenty-four hours on the ribs to help with the pain. My experience with this pain is very good. It is nothing compared to my leg last June. As a matter of fact, my leg hurts more right now than my ribs do!

I do have a hard time with narcotics. This time, the meds gave me tinnitus (ringing in my ears) and sensitivity to loud talk or noises. I hope it goes away as we reduce the meds.

The nursing care at St. Francis was top-notch. If I rang the buzzer for a nurse or assistant, I was speaking to someone within ten to fifteen seconds, and I had someone in the room soon after that. I have never had better nursing service. I was almost embarrassed to bother them as I felt so well. Only one of my caregivers seemed "detached" and a bit tentative. Unfortunately, she was also the nurse who catheterized me—ouch! That is another story.

WRITTEN APRIL 3, 2011, 4:31 P.M.

This has been a confusing two days since I got home from St. Francis Hospital. I started on painkillers that the doctors thought I would surely need, given the rib involvement in this operation. When I started taking them Friday and Saturday, they were much too strong for me. I was reduced to a confused state of mind with ringing in my ears and zero understanding of what was happening to me. I backed way off the drugs and felt much more normal last night.

I was supposed to take painkillers every twelve hours (for OxyContin) and every four hours (for Percocet). I backed off to one Percocet tablet before bed and slept until about 5:30 a.m. this morning and woke up very sore. Okay, so I needed a bit more pain relief. I took a Percocet midmorning. An incredible tiredness came over me, and I slept right though the morning. I woke up for maybe a half hour of "drunk with sleep" conversation with Cindy when she got home from church, and then I fell asleep for two and a half hours this afternoon, waking up still tired. Anyone have an opinion about all this sleep and drowsiness?

WRITTEN APRIL 4, 2011, 8:49 A.M.

Thank you for your comments on the fatigue and sleep issues. It was good to know that I could throw a question out there and benefit from the life experiences that so many of you have had. I try to reason myself through this whole thing, and sometimes I come up in a pity party. I think I have a healthy attitude about what is happening, but there are times when I feel very much like a scared little boy searching for his mama. This little give-and-take in the last twenty-four hours was most helpful, just knowing that someone was listening. Thank you, all.

WRITTEN APRIL 5, 2011, 4:47 A.M.

Later today ,an old friend (since 1977) will be visiting. Her husband, Richard, died from cancer last July. Cindy and I attended their Quaker wedding in Vermont, but we missed his funeral because of my own sickness. I am looking forward to seeing Beth. She has wisdom beyond her years and has coped with serious illness. I just want you all to know that I have some of the greatest friends any man could ever wish for. God has taken care of Capt. Bob in that area. I am daily amazed by the calls and visits that I get. My prayer is that I can be as good a friend to you as you have been to me.

The fatigue continues but not as profoundly as a couple of days ago. Today, I have an appointment for blood testing. We will see how it is afterward. I am trying to sit more each day. The doctors, among other things, warn of pneumonia and want me to stay vertical given a choice.

Last night, we dined on yet another meal brought in by a friend. The simple kindness of a meal can only be fully appreciated from the receiving side. Each gift is more time that I have with my soul mate, Cindy. She works so hard to make everyone happy. I am thankful when she is made happy herself. Last night, she struggled to remain awake for the UConn men's win. Cindy had been up since about 2:00 a.m. the night before as she could not sleep.

WRITTEN APRIL 6, 2011, 8:29 P.M.

Well, the UConn women finally lost. The men won it all in the NCAA tournament, and I think I rounded a corner in my recovery from this latest surgery. It has surprised me how differently the same drugs can react in the same body a year apart. I think I have the combination I need right now. It has been a week today since my surgery, and I can attest to you that the rib cage can be a very tender area. It is essential that the postoperative patient not breath, sneeze, cough, try to get themselves up, bend over to tie shoes, try to use the toilet, or bump into anything. Control those things, and it's a snap. LOL

The mental battle is easier when you can think straight, which is when you are in pain without drugs. So what happens is that your mood never swings toward good. You are either in pain and don't want to be bothered or not in pain and drugged up and bad company. Cindy should get an award for this one.

I think I will get to church this weekend. At least that is my goal. Stitches come out next Monday—always a welcome event. Everything kind of pulls one or another of the incisions. Sleep is on my back only, not a native position for me.

Got a phone call today from one of our Bible study groups from church, and they have set it up to come out to my house on Saturday to rake up for spring. That is one of the nicest things that someone could do for me right now. I live on the side of a hill and walking is very slow and not very safe for me since the leg operation last June. Cindy and I love our church (www.fellowshipchurchct.com), and things like this are just good examples of people living their faith, not just professing it. Thanks in advance, guys. I will pray for good weather. I hope everyone is having a good week. See you all later.

Written April 11, 2011, 6:01 p.m.

I am officially in the dumps. I will snap out of it with His help, but I am bummed out.

We had an appointment to have the stitches removed today from my last surgery ten days ago. The healing is going well, but I am still uncomfortable mid to late afternoon. I am using Percocet as needed. The doctor pulled the stitches and released me from his care, referring me back to my original surgeon, who worked on my leg last year. He also gave me a two-page report on the biopsy done to the lung tissue removed ten days ago.

The human mind is a wonderful thing. When there is a test being done, we can hold ourselves together with hope, trust, love, or as in my case, with just plain orneriness. My trick is to not allow myself to dwell on something that is too big for me to wrap my arms around. I take little bites out of it. It takes a while, but I get it down.

So the tests came back that the cancer removed from my right lung was spawned by the cancer in my leg. It is a metastatic malignant fibrous histiocytoma, and there are no guarantees that this one instance is all there will be. In the operation, the doctor sectioned a lung lobe and sent it off to the lab. The report, all two pages of it, used clinical language as expected, but translated, it comes out that this was a "vigorously" growing cancer with many giant cells, which offers a poor prognosis.

I will be testing every ninety days to find out if further surgery is needed. Oh and I forgot to mention, this "rare" cancer does not usually respond to radiation or chemo therapy.

WRITTEN APRIL 13, 2011, 10:59 P.M.

If you read the last several pages of the "guestbook" comments on this site, it is impossible to say that I am not a blessed man. Each of you in your own way has reached out to me, extending encouragement, a prayer, or an offer to assist. I have even been taken behind the woodshed by people who know me well and who can jolt me back into reality. (Thank you, Judy.) It is humbling beyond description to know that I have so many great people who are sharing the burden I carry. I was rocked pretty good by these last few weeks. I did not expect the lingering discomfort after I had done so well in the hospital, and I started feeling a little sorry for myself. I don't know what I thought the biopsy report would say, but I was not ready for the hard copy. Strangely, I think I was strengthened by the ordeal and certainly blown away with the response from you, my friends.

I was not in favor of this CaringBridge stuff when my daughter, Erica, suggested it. She had a friend who used it while the woman was going through treatment for breast cancer. CaringBridge worked for her as it is working for me, and she has beaten the disease so far. The "give and take" here has been a medicine for not only the body but also the soul. Sometimes "His love which passes all understanding" is the only crutch that I can lean on. The mind is a strange and wonderful thing but knows where it can inflict exquisite pain. It knows your deepest secrets and weakest points. My mind snuck up on me last week, and it has taken me until tonight when I was in prayer with my men's Bible study to gain a feeling of elation spreading through me again. God just needed to be asked into the match again.

I find that I can share details here that under normal circumstance would be too private for printed word. CaringBridge seems to have a cathartic effect on me. After all, the blog is the perfect listener to my problems. I have trusted you who are reading this, and you have trusted me with your responses. It would be a great thing for us all to be more like this when a crisis is not the reason for our transparency. I thank you for your bravery to write. It may actually be easier for me than it is for you.

Bob

Chapter 7

Happy for Boredom

NOTHING HAPPENED ... NICE!

WRITTEN APRIL 22, 2011, 9:07 P.M.

What a nice week. Nothing happened—nothing, nada, nix. I loved it. I worked on my new hobby of playing the ukulele and am developing nice calluses on the fingertips of my left hand. Things are going well with the "uke." I am training my fingers to move from chord to chord and very encouraged with what I have learned. The "hokey" sound from the uke can be quite nice to play, and there are many songs adapted for its use. I am using a book called *The Daily Ukulele*, and it contains 365 songs, one for each day of the year. I can get through about twenty of them so far. Notice that I said "get through." I didn't say "play." I have to develop more speed in changing from chord to chord. On a uke you can have a chord for each syllable of a word, and some of the chords are real finger twisters.

Had an echocardiogram this week after being reminded by one of those automated phone messaging systems. I had forgotten all about that. Next week, back to my surgeon for an in-depth discussion of the biopsy report. I think I will have a few important questions to ask him about that.

My ribs—no, rather my stomach muscles—are still sore. It is a constantly nagging type of pain that is exacerbated only when the grandkids jump me from the right side. Then it smarts. I am not sure why the stomach muscles should hurt when the ribs themselves, which everyone told me were going to smart, seem perfectly okay. When I asked the cardiothoracic surgeon about that, he mentioned that he had to cut through three muscles to get to my lung and that they were connected. I still don't understand why muscles ten to twelve inches away from the nearest incision should ache. It is not bad enough to take painkillers but bothersome as it is always there.

My family and I are looking so forward to Easter Sunday! It is my favorite church day of the year and the basis for my entire faith. We had the grandkids over tonight to celebrate our first annual Good Friday dinner and egg-coloring session. We read from Bennett's Boys Bible and also from a lighthearted Easter storybook that Sadie owns. It was fun because Bennett read it to us. It is amazing how much Bennett understands about the Easter story and the gospels depicting it. He told me all about doubting Thomas and the proof that he needed in order to believe. Are you a doubting Thomas? I was. It took a book by Lee Strobel titled *A Case for Christ* to convince me that it was easier to believe in the Bible and Christ and all He said than to believe in the big bang theory.

WRITTEN MAY 16, 2011, 11:23 P.M.

Sorry to take so long getting back to the blog. I don't have lots to report. I am now in a waiting game with this disease. It's not fun, but life is wonderful.

After my lung surgery, I had been preparing for my visit with my cancer surgeon, Dr. S, for several weeks. I had the full copy of the biopsy report from my surgery laid out near my computer, and I had been trying to find something that sounded good; however, I mostly confused myself. I did prepare several questions for him, but really, I was just looking forward to sitting down and getting the straight scoop right from the source. He really didn't tell me anything that I didn't already suspect, but he did clarify aspects of my treatment. I like this guy because he pulls no punches and answers my questions directly. Here is what he had to say.

1. The cancer is an invasive stage-four metastatic spindle cell sarcoma, also called a malignant fibrous histiocytoma. It is a type of sarcoma.

2. It moved to my right lung from my leg. (Eighty percent of these cancers appear somewhere in the soft tissue of the body and then appear in the lung, and they may also migrate to the liver. The cancer moves through the bloodstream.)

3. The leg (saved in 2010 by an operation in June) and my recent MRI show no further cancer growth at the primary location.

4. In March, my ninety-day routine scan showed the cancer in my right lung.

5. An operation on March 30 resulted in a triangular sectioning of my right lung and the removal of a small tumor. This was done through three incisions between my ribs (ouch!). I am back on my feet from this operation now (5/5/2011).

My consultation yielded the following additional information:

1. The tumor in the lung was growing aggressively but successfully removed.

2. Because it was fast-growing and had numerous giant cells, there is added concern for reoccurrences.

3. The doctor is stepping up the ninety-day scans. Instead of alternating X-rays (low radiation) with CT scans (high radiation), I will be getting only CT scans every ninety days. They are now less concerned with the additional radiation and risk of long-term cancers that the CT scans can cause. (As a point of information, one chest CT scan is around ten millisieverts of radiation, and a traditional chest X-ray is only 0.02 millisieverts. A CT scan delivers five hundred times the radiation of an X-ray. Lifetime maximum recommended levels are a hundred millisieverts or ten CT scans.) I have had four CT scans to date.

4. If the cancer reappears in the lung, I can probably have another operation like the one I had in March.

5. If the cancer appears in multiple locations in the lung at the same time, it could be labeled "inoperable."

6. Having said all that, I am currently cancer-free and hope to stay that way. My CT scan, coming up on June 30th, is the next hurtle.

I am pleased with what the human spirit can handle when push comes to shove. I continue to trust in God and know that He has a plan for me. I pray with confidence for a cure, and I understand that I do not control the outcome, He does. Sometimes I get hung up on not being worthy of God's healing, but then I remember that I was not worthy of my redemption either when He gave His Son for my sins (and yours) freely. I am not afraid because I am not alone. He is always with me.

I have been blessed with a wonderful life, great kids and stepkids, fabulous grandchildren, and the greatest gift a man could ever have, a loving wife who is also my best friend. You can bet that I am looking forward to remaining cancer-free, but this thing is not going to screw up the rest of my life regardless of how things go.

WRITTEN JUNE 26, 2011, 7:10 P.M.

I haven't written in the journal for some time now as everything seems to be going rather smoothly. For the past two months or so, my little job as registrar of voters for Durham has gone well, and I even received a framed award when I was at a political dinner. They found out that campaign finance laws would be a problem if they only honored one person, so three additional people were feted. I was one of them. It was pretty funny.

I had great fun helping out the Valley Railroad with some clerical items needed by the US Coast Guard. We prepped for an inspection that was held last week. Now that was really something, as our riverboat was inspected by four children from the CG. LOL

My volunteer work at church has ramped up recently as I lead the buildings and grounds committee, and we are about to spend a significant amount of money on our teens environment. Our committee is currently working on a new electrical service for our updated stage area—installing sound-dampening panels to quiet down the echoes and resurfacing the room's floor. The room is fifty-eight feet wide by ninety-eight feet long, with a thirty-foot ceiling. It used to be a gymnasium, not a sound stage. We also are renovating three classrooms to become a meeting area/office space.

My next cancer scan is this coming Thursday (6/30/2011). I have one every ninety days. This is the first of what I hope are many. I can count on one hand the times when I have thought seriously about this scan, but as it comes closer, I am feeling some butterfly activity. Whenever I feel that way, I look *up*.

I will post a journal entry Thursday evening to let you guys know how it goes. I get the results of the CT scan immediately. Your prayers are always welcomed. Please know that I am also praying for you. I pray you have wonderful childhoods, tolerable siblings, wonderful marriages, kids, and grandchildren if you want them. My Cole, Lara, Bennett, and Sadie are the sparkles in my eyes. They have dotted the I's and slashed the T's on a wonderful life.

Talk to you soon.

GOOD NEWS!

WRITTEN JUNE 30, 2011, 6:39 P.M.

I got good news today. There was no change in my CT scan from last time. I have a lot to tell you but have no time right now. My stepdaughter just arrived with wine and cannoli, so it is time to celebrate a little. I will be back with more on this.

WRITTEN JULY 2, 2011, 1:07 A.M.

My wife, Cindy, was taken by ambulance to the Middlesex Memorial Hospital this morning at 9:00, suffering from dizziness, nausea, and confusion. At first, doctors thought that her problem was stress-related (my illness and the cancer scan that I had on yesterday that came back clean), but by tonight, they are thinking it may have been a stroke.

Cindy initially had a memory loss, but thankfully, all of her memory returned by about 5:00 p.m. tonight. The continuing nausea and vertigo points to stroke, but we will not have an MRI (which should give the doctors the specific information that they need to determine the cause) until sometime Saturday morning. She is alert, resting, and looking forward to losing "that last five pounds" as she cannot keep anything down right now.

As always, her spirit is not defeated, and she is the bright and caring person you all know her to be.

It has been super busy here, but I thought that I should come to you with this information and ask my prayer partners to place a call to God for His intervention and healing with Cindy's illness. I ask your prayers at this time for her fast recovery.

Bob

YOU WON'T BELIEVE THIS ONE!

WRITTEN JULY 2, 2011, 7:26 P.M.

I don't know how to tell you what has been going on here. It is beyond confusing. I am just really happy that my stepdaughter, Vicki, was on board to see and hear all of the craziness Cindy has been enduring at the hospital.

Let me cut to the quick. Cindy did not have a stroke or a TIA. We just got home, and she is resting. The hospital ran many thousands of dollars' worth of tests and came up utterly, totally, unabashedly scratching their heads. At first it was maybe stress, then maybe her MS, and then maybe TIA or stroke. Then early Alzheimer was mentioned. Then transient amnesia.

As she was being released from the hospital, here is what the last doctor told us he thought it was: "An episode caused by a chemical imbalance in the brain that corrected itself over the past two days." Here is the best part! He went on to blame the Chinese food, wine and cannoli that we ate after the good news about my cancer scan. As God is my witness, I am telling you the truth! Totally insane!

We are left now to follow up with Cindy's specialists after the weekend. Between now and then, we are taking care to give her plenty of rest. We will be missing church tomorrow to be on the safe side. Debbie will be visiting to fill us in afterward.

WRITTEN JULY 15, 2011, 5:25 P.M.

Things are back to "normal." Cindy's very scary episode turned out to be "transient global amnesia" (TGA), which is caused by stress in women and by physical exertion in men.

We got the good news about my cancer scan, and the next morning, Cindy had her amnesia and dizziness. Bottom line is that her body crashed and she needed to do a reboot. She is fine now and plans to take meds to support her during the tension-filled last week or so of the ninety-day cycle of cancer scans that I will be having for the rest of my life. The TGA is not supposed to repeat, but we are taking no chances. Now that it is over, we can laugh a bit about it. Cindy was funny as she could not remember where she kept her clothes. (By the way, I am still getting flack from her for the ensemble I dressed her in before the ambulance got to our house.) She did not remember that I had cancer. She did not remember the scan the previous day. She remembered she had a PT appointment at Gaylord Hospital, but she could not remember what Gaylord was, where it was, or how to get there. She could not recall who her doctor was, but she nicely asked over and over for chocolate. Repetitive statements are a symptom of TGA.

So we are both fine now, and we are counting down the eighty or so days left for my next scan. Life is good. The grandkids are great. My kids are flying in for a week-long visit this weekend, and the pool is open.

I have been counting my blessings, and they pretty much are composed of memories of family and friends, places I have sailed to, and the one woman who has loved me for thirty years this coming August.

IT'S JUST ME AGAIN.

WRITTEN SEP. 27, 2011, 12:16 A.M.

I have not written in a while, and that is good. Life has been kind, and with the exception of my handicap (difficulty walking) and my natural aging process, I have enjoyed it immensely. Cindy does not show any remnants of her amnesia scare, and darn, she remembers all of my miscues, even from years ago. LOL.

During late June and through July and August, I was fortunate to be able to get deeply involved in some remodeling work at church. I did do some light work, mostly in a stationary position, sometimes up on a hydraulic lift thirty feet in the air. More importantly, I was trusted with pulling together the organization and the implementation of the rebuild. Thank you to the volunteers who made the job possible in the allotted time. We converted a gymnasium into a youth center, changing out the overhead lights, rewiring the room, and installing commercial sound panels suspended from the ceiling to break up the echoes that are produced by hard surfaces. The youth group is called Living Proof, and I was delighted to attend the grand opening of the facility last Friday evening.

Check us out at http://www.iamlivingproof.net.

My consulting at the Valley Railroad was really fun, and we had a very good emergency exercise with fire boats from five local towns participating. The largest one was a brand new boat from Old Saybrook, which cost $250,000!

With US Coast Guard officials looking on, we simulated a fire, two man-overboards, and an unruly crowd, and maybe even a heart attack got thrown in there. Congrats to Captain Dave for doing a great job, given the pandemonium. The purpose of the exercise is to stress the "best made plans of mice and men" beyond their breaking points and learn from our mistakes. My hat is also off to our lead, Captain Paul C., who has taken over my responsibilities for running the exercises and who is doing a great job. I hope I have a place in next year's program with the US Coast Guard. Heck, I hope I have a part in next year.

My childhood friend Paul and his wife visited for a week in September, and it was good to catch up as well as reminisce about our "Black Cat Club" and "Women Haters Society." We were about ten years old then, and things have changed.

I scared myself silly last week as I was having a little difficulty breathing and I had a sharp pain in my chest from time to time. I also coughed up quite a bit. I immediately thought of the "C" word and that it might be coming back. Cindy has the discomfort now and a cough to boot, so I guess it is something contagious and nothing to worry about. One of my doctors is monitoring my oxygen levels overnight on Friday. Maybe I will know more about this thing then.

I am breathing much better and conclude that I must be finishing up a bad chest cold. That is the worst about my situation. When you don't feel well, you wind up tying yourself up in knots wondering—

My next CT scan is due in late October. I hope I don't have to talk to you again until then. By the way, thanks for staying tuned in. I hope you never have to find out how comforting a blog like this is.

I would like to share a couple of Bible verses with you today:

Therefore we do not lose heart. Though outwardly we are wasting away, yet inwardly we are being renewed day by day. For our light and momentary troubles are achieving for us an eternal glory that far outweighs them all. So we fix our eyes not on what is seen, but on what is unseen. For what is seen is temporary, but what is unseen is eternal. (2 Corinthians 4:16–18 (NASB))

God bless you all.

Capt. Bob

Chapter 8

ON MY BACK AGAIN

WRITTEN OCTOBER 3, 2011, 7:21 P.M.

My breathing didn't get any better, and Cindy pretty much demanded that I go to the doctor. I called him at 2:00 p.m. today, and they gave me an appointment for 3:40 p.m. My oxygen saturation was tested over the weekend by a device that I wore overnight. It showed that my oxygen level dropped to under 80 percent three different times overnight and was accompanied by rapid heartbeats. I had a chest X-ray, and what do you know, my right lung was filling with liquid. At least I had good reason to struggle for air. The X-ray was taken at 5:00 p.m., and the doctor would not let me leave until he spoke to my breathing specialist. They think it may be pneumonia or perhaps my heart disease popping up. Blood tests tomorrow should tell. Meanwhile, I will be getting a machine to use at night along with my BiPAP breather, which feeds oxygen into my face mask. It should make my sleeping tolerable. Right now as I type this, my chest is heaving, trying to get enough oxygen. It is not a comfortable thing but bearable at this level. Much worse and it's the hospital for me until they remedy this fluid thing.

I guess I will go back to more frequent blogs to keep you up to date.

TUESDAY NIGHT!

WRITTEN OCTOBER 4, 2011, 8:02 P.M.

My bedroom sounds like the inside of a factory. The oxygen accumulator is a large suitcase-sized device that takes air and strips out the oxygen and then pumps that O2 into my sleep apnea device. I am very glad to be able to breathe again. Combining the extra O2 with doubled-up diuretics and a big cutback in liquids, I should be feeling better soon. The pulmonary doctor is waiting to hear what my cardiologist will say on Thursday afternoon, and both of them are also waiting for my next CT scan, which is setup for next Tuesday. At this point, we all hope that this issue is merely a symptom of my CHF (congestive heart failure). CHF really does not kill you until later on, but it must be monitored closely. I literally cannot do a thing. After I finished eating a small supper and using the head, I was so out of breath that it took a half hour on the machine to restore comfort.

The other possibility for all this is cancer again in that lung.

I ask for your prayers over the next week until my CT scan. I will be one happy camper if I am clean.

IT'S NOW A DISNEY E TICKET RIDE.

WRITTEN OCTOBER 5, 2011, 4:32 P.M.

It is scary when you get a lot of attention from multiple doctors. I had been instructed to call my pulmonary doctor today to get my blood test results.

The results were not what he expected, and they did not resolve what is going on. Dr. P asked me to not wait until next Tuesday for a CT scan but instead to go in immediately and get one done. Immediately turns out to be tomorrow at 11:00 a.m., and it will be a double dose of radiation—once without and once with contrasting agents in my blood. The rush-rush reason for the test is because one of the things that could be doing this to me is a blood clot. If it were to break loose, bad things could happen. The other unfortunate possibility is a return of the cancer. I don't know if anything good could come out from this test, but we are praying for it.

Sorry to be burdening you all of a sudden with this stuff, but I do so wish to share with my friends where my head really is and the comfort that I receive from my strong faith in Jesus Christ through this whole thing. The idea of handling this situation without God is inconceivable to me. The comfort I receive from Him is palpable. I can touch it, and I have no fear.

I appreciate your interest in this blog, but do not worry about me. I pray that you will have the same blessings and strength as I have when it is your turn to deal with problems that will surely happen.

Cindy continues to be a rock. I never have deserved her, but I thank God daily for a loving wife.

More news tomorrow after the CT scan results.

ST. FRANCIS HOSPITAL

WRITTEN OCTOBER 6, 2011, 8:29 P.M.

After visits to multiple doctors' office today and two CT scans, I was admitted to St. Francis Hospital for an operation on my lung scheduled for tomorrow morning 8:00 a.m. The operation will do two things: (1) it will remove all of the liquid that currently surrounds my right lung (this liquid has made it very difficult to breathe) and (2) it will determine whether the liquid surrounding the lung in cancerous.

We need prayers for a real miracle. But please remember to pray that it be the will of God.

Thanks in advance for your prayers. Look forward to seeing you guys.

PS: Please remember to support the MAPS Wheelathon/Walkathon on October 16. At this point, I plan to be there to walk that quarter-mile route.

WRITTEN OCTOBER 8, 2011, 8:22 P.M. BY CINDY SCHULTE

Sorry for the delay, guys. This is Cindy writing this as Bob is still in the hospital. The sad news is that the fluid around the lung was cancerous. The good news is that Bob is in good spirits. He is confident that God is in control, and we'll find out as we go along what the next step is. For now, we'll keep taking those prayers for the will of God and know that we are doing fine.

I am so pleased with all that our family is right there for us. Just know that when Bob gets out of St. Francis, he will have touched many. Handing out the cards, Andy.

God bless you all. I am checking out my DVR tonight. There are some shows to watch.

Cindy

WRITTEN OCTOBER 10, 2011, 6:35 P.M.

I was allowed to leave St. Francis hospital in Hartford today. I underwent a somewhat difficult procedure called chemical pleurodesis. During this procedure, a chemical is injected into the pleural space to permanently seal the two layers of the pleura together. This may help prevent further fluid buildup. This operation allowed the doctors to sort out what is going on in my chest and give me the long-term prognosis as they see it.

But please ... let's start in the beginning and follow these last few days out. On last Wednesday (10/29/2011), my thoracic surgeon insisted he needed a CT scan in order to get a really good picture of my lung. CT scans are not something I readily agree to, as the radiation load is significant. I called my thoracic surgeon back and asked if he could wait until next Tuesday to get the information. The surgeon politely refused and asked that I not only move up the CT scan to immediately but also get two scans—one scan without dye and one with—so that even shadowy images would become ultra clear to the naked eye. We went forward immediately and scored an appointment for October 6, last Thursday. I called my Dr. "Cancer." He immediately gave me an appointment following the CT scan in Hartford. He wanted to see it first. Heck, I wanted him to see it first as well. I needed to push back my cardiologist appointment for later on in the afternoon to accommodate the new surgeon's appointment. Dr. Cancer read the file and immediately called the head thoracic surgeon in St. Francis. He was the man who "did" my lung last March. I love him and call him Dr. Lungs.

Dr. Lungs was in his office in St. Francis, one floor down and about twenty suites to the left. Down we went, and before the day was out, I was admitted to the hospital and was being prepped for surgery. I was very happy that I always took my mother's advice and wore clean underwear whenever I went somewhere, nice navy blue checkered, which complimented my eyes. Oxygen was begun, and I settled into Room 8922, I finally could breathe again. The next morning, Friday the 7th, I was operated on, and answers finally became available.

The cancer has spread to the lymph system and could break out anywhere. The bottom line is that it is terminal cancer and that I can expect the end sooner than later. Now that is probably shocking to some of you. I promise an increasingly spiritual blog next time as we delve into the frailties of man and the generosity of God. We are fine, but nobody—and I mean nobody—understands why. I will be in touch.

Written October 11, 2011, 8:01 a.m.

I have thought about how the format of this blog should work in the future. Up until now, I have reported usually on an event, and you have read and responded with encouragement. I am not sure that will work much longer as I think I may be running out of newsworthy events. I am clearly in survival mode and trying to pass my remaining time with an eye toward "quality of life."

Over the past months, God has been present with me at a "palpable" level. He has offered me encouragement, great tranquility, and courage far beyond Bob Schulte. I feel God's presence with me and have gone so far as to introduce Him as a member of the group when people visit. (Yes, this seems very crazy.) I have not repeated the thoughts that have come into my mind, except to a few trusted churchmen. I wanted to see how it felt to be sure. I did not want to get melodramatic. The thoughts God gave me are His. I was afraid to discuss them as it was such a pompous idea and not something someone would associate with Bob Schulte. Now that the direction of things is clear, I will risk sharing with you these thoughts that have haunted me for several weeks, and I consider them a gift of God.

"I believe that God is asking me to be an example in death so that others may find Him and gain eternal life."

In my first journal entry, I asked about cancer: "Why me, Lord? Why not me?"

Now I ask the same question about my salvation. "Why did You save me, Lord? Why me?" This question deserves a spiritual answer, and I think His wanting me to be an example fits. Any thoughts?

WRITTEN OCTOBER 12, 2011, 12:09 A.M.

Thank you, Cole and Lara, for writing in my guestbook. To those who do not know, Cole and Lara are my grandchildren in Minneapolis. I thank God every day for your lives and your love. I would love to be able to chop down a tree with you. I hope you can visit around Christmas. I pray that all grandparents get to know and enjoy their grandchildren. When I want warm fuzzies, I don't think about old jobs I have had or any business accomplishments. My fuzzies come named Cole, Lara, Bennett, and Sadie. They are my greatest success. Thanks for letting me rave.

OXYGEN IS A GOOD THING.

WRITTEN OCTOBER 13, 2011, 8:53 A.M.

I feel as well prepared as anyone to deal with this terminal phase. My heart, which has been an issue now for six or seven years, is now in atrial fibrillation mode. It beats pretty randomly, and oxygen absorption is not good. The result is my using oxygen much of the time (a pain in the butt) and unfortunately a clear knowledge of the condition I am in with every breath.

I know about pain. I had great pain when my leg was first reconstructed back in June of 2010. I managed it when it was acute and was quickly able to refuse the painkillers. They made me wacky, and I did not like the lack of control.

Breathing is something else. Something so natural, but so scary when you feel like you cannot get the O2 you need. The other night, one of my machines was unplugged from the outlet, and I woke up in an oxygen-deprived state, deeply breathing CO_2 into my sleep mask and rebreathing the stale air. I sat upright in bed for a half hour in this state until Cindy came in and found I was unplugged. Cindy plugged me back in. I was asleep in a half hour and slept peacefully another four hours. Have I ever told you, Cindy, that you are my hero?

SUNDAY WHEEL-A-THON, WALK-A-THON.

WRITTEN OCTOBER 13, 2011, 8:10 P.M.

Okay, so here is my last mention of this special event taking place at Xavier High School's track right behind the school on Randolph Road in Middletown at 9:30 a.m. until 3:00 p.m. on October 16th.

Participants will register and walk or wheelchair around the quarter-mile track for the benefit of patients with multiple sclerosis served by our MAPS (Middlesex Area Patient Services) group. Some of our patients are coming to try to get around themselves, and some may ask volunteers for a push. I will be there and plan to get around that track, perhaps with the help of my two grandchildren, Bennett and Sadie, or perhaps by dragging my walker around with me and stopping to rest every seventy-five feet or so. Times do not matter. One lap or ten, drop in a donation or write a check. We need it badly this year, and the economy hurts charities at least as much as the rest of us.

So here is a challenge: If I can make it around the track once, why can't you? How about taking the family around once and make a small collective gift?

Bring a camera. It should be sweet.

SHOUT-OUT TO ANITA

WRITTEN OCTOBER 13, 2011, 8:25 P.M.

Anita, your entry brings me great joy. We grew up in the best of times, the 50s. Girls were princesses, and boys were cowboys. There was a great and long childhood innocence. Heck, I didn't know anything about sex until Gregory Gospel told me about it in eighth grade! I treasure those times and can say that I loved you then with a more chaste love than exists today. Thank you for being my first gal. Thank you for the balloon dance in 1958 and then again fifty years later in the same auditorium within ten feet of the same spot as near as I can remember. No one wants to die, and there are times when the evil one tries to get me to fail in my walk with Jesus. I need your prayers and ask all those reading my blog to pray that God's will be done with me and that I "finish well." The dance was called a balloon dance because we boys could not physically touch the girls back then. Hands had to be kept behind your back!

RAINY DAY FRIDAY

WRITTEN OCTOBER 14, 2011, 3:21 P.M.

Wow! Wind, rain, blown leaves and branches, it's really wild out there. Glad I didn't have to go out in it. Bennett used to be bothered by strong winds, but now it seems as though he doesn't much care.

Over the years when it has been windy, my mind sometimes would wander to my sailing days. There were times when we were racing that we carried way too much sail for the conditions, but we sure did fly downwind. I remember one race from Old Saybrook to Block Island in which we carried a reaching spinnaker right past race rock in 56-knot winds. I still have a four-by-six-foot B&W photo covering one wall of Cindy's office. It was a "feeder" race for Block Island Race Week, and *Yachting Magazine* was out photographing the nuts that participated.

My boat at the time was a 1976 Morgan 27 racer designed by Charles Morgan. It was called a quarter-ton MORC ocean racer and was the fastest twenty-seven-footer in the world from 1972 until about 1974. She was built just before the ultralights started to make their presence felt. Her name was the *Restless III*, named after Adrian Block's *Onrust* (translation restless), in which he found the Connecticut River, Block Island, and Fisher's Island.

I am looking forward to a visit on Saturday from my New Jersey relatives. All the nephews and nieces are grown up with families of their own. It is an honor to think that they would come up here, which is more than three hours each way, to visit with their Uncle Bob. My family is the best.

WHEEL-A-THON, WALK-A-THON SUCCESS!

WRITTEN OCTOBER 16, 2011, 7:11 P.M.

I am deeply moved by the show of support that Cindy and I received from our friends, relatives and church people. The MAPS (Middlesex Area Patient Services) fundraiser was brand new to us this year, and it was a resounding success, raising over $3,000.00 for this wonderful small charity that benefits MS patients locally.

Thank you Xavier High School for the great track, high-jump area, and pole vault pit. The Pancoast boys were in the house!

Thank you, God, for the weather and your blessings on our day.

WRITTEN OCTOBER 17, 2011, 5:27 P.M.

Here it is, Monday evening. Cindy is not home yet from meeting the grandchildren's bus. Supper will be simple tonight as we had some dynamite eggplant for lunch, and cereal with blueberries sounds just great to me. We picked the blueberries at Lyman Orchards with all four grandchildren a couple of months ago. Sometimes luxuries are as simple as handpicked berries. I am glad I still appreciate that kind of thing. Life is full of wonders that are free. I won't bother you with my list. It is more important that I know I can come up with a list a mile long. How about you? Did you ever think that you should step off the world's ladder for a minute and just enjoy. When I look left and right and behind, I see only the important things in my life—children, grandchildren, siblings, special gatherings, birthday parties, weddings, Thanksgiving on the Cape, and always Christmas at home. *Always* Christmas at home.

Along the way, I have met many wonderful people, some from schools, neighborhoods, and church. I probably will never be able to thank everyone for their friendship and love, but I hope that you know who you are. I hope you know I loved you as children of God and participants in my life. I loved you for the journey we take together in this life. We are soul mates.

I have found out that I have an expiration date coming up. Gee whiz, I am not going to live forever. I'm not stupid. I knew that, but so much of my life was lived as if I was the star of the show and nothing could take me down. Life's speed bumps showed me otherwise. We all experience trials and tribulations in our lives. It is humbling when the wrinkles set in. The belts can't control the roll, and life is no longer a wild ride. Thoughts of eternity become a big part of your thought process. God becomes someone of interest, and the terrible tug-of-war with the Devil gains strength. Do you believe, or don't you? Are you willing to face the consequences that go along with belief? Can you forgive a sibling or good friend who did you wrong? How about that first wife? Can you clean up your act so that it could be played out on a stage for all to see and judge? Can you get that good?

I am sitting here in the powerful position of having a strong following of friends who love me and read my blog faithfully. I just called it my blog. Well, it really isn't. It is our blog. You wouldn't be reading it if you weren't interested in the outcome or the journey. I am stripping naked in front of you because I think that I have found something that can help you with your own journey. My prayers started off specific: "Save me!" They have now changed dramatically and ask only that God's will be done. I surrender completely to Him and in return find myself immersed in grace and love from Jesus that I cannot describe except to say it feels very much like being rocked in your mom's arms as a child. I don't consider myself especially brave, so where is this strength coming from? It comes from grace, which is being heaped upon me. I am buried in it. I still feel. I still fear, but I cannot imagine what it would be like without grace. When I put my head down on my pillow at night and am vulnerable to the terrible thoughts, I celebrate the peace that I receive from Jesus Christ.

I wouldn't change this feeling for the world.

CARDIOLOGIST'S VISIT

WRITTEN OCTOBER 18, 2011, 10:10 P.M.

I have had atrial fibrillation for about seven years that I know of and perhaps longer but not recognized. Sinus rhythm is normal heartbeat—a nice lub-dub sound. When someone is in "A-fib," the heart has an erratic beat caused by electrical pulses being produced by the atrium, a small chamber at the very beginning of the heart.

The atrium should squeeze just before the ventricle does the big work of forcing blood throughout your body. The idea is to "top off" the ventricle with blood from the atrium just before it fires so the maximum amount of blood flows with the least effort. If the atrium is out of time, then blood flow is reduced accordingly. Combine poor blood flow with lack of oxygenation, and you can feel quite miserable with A-fib. My A-fib has been controlled by drugs until now. Now I have had two serious lung operations, and the heart-lung combo doesn't like what is going on. My cardiologist now tells me he is treating me to minimize symptoms and does not reasonably think that he can "stop" the A-fib for good. In three to four weeks, if my blood-thinner level is maintained, I will be wheeled into an outpatient facility and anesthetized for several minutes. During that time, they will stop my heart and then electrically start it again with electrical pads. Dr. Cardio hopes that it will stay in sinus rhythm for a meaningful amount of time. Most of the exhaustion that I am experiencing relates to the A-fib (followed by the cancer). Dr. Cardio also reported that there did not seem to be too much liquid back in my chest cavity. I had hoped for none.

Our lawyer visited us at home early Tuesday, and before 10:00, he had what he needed to draw up a new will for us. He will also draw up living wills and powers of attorney. Nice guy but morbid stuff.

I appreciate greatly the words of encouragement that I receive from you guys. That Bob Schulte you guys mention in your postings seems like a great guy. Do I know him? I don't necessarily feel like the guy you are speaking of. I have all of the same fears that anyone would have going through an end-of-life sickness. I have regrets that I needed to forgive myself for and many things that I didn't do well in life. I think I am pretty average. I like to say that I am just a survivor going through the "bumper car" ride called life. I am not especially proud of the fact that I was fifty-five years old before I found my way into a lasting relationship with Christ. Having said that, the fact that Christ didn't give up on me amazes me. His gift of salvation, given long ago, still impacts lives like mine today. When I truly understood that some years ago, I wept uncontrollably. He has given me the grace to face this challenge. This isn't Bob Schulte handling death. This is Jesus carrying me through this thing. Yes, I have been given the gift of understanding, but the courage is not mine. I am a coward.

One of the big ah-ha's that I have had is that God gives us grace in return for our gift to Him of our faith. Believe hard and receive tenfold grace. Call it a system if you want, but it works for me. Jesus has not left my side in weeks. It is marvelously Him, not Bob Schulte sharing Himself with you and using my situation as a parable in the modern age.

WRITTEN OCTOBER 23, 2011, 9:42 P.M.

This week has been a busy one! I had four important meetings with doctors and now have a better handle on things. I won't get into detailed descriptions, but here is a thumbnail summary. My breathing doctor would love for me to go down to Sloan-Kettering in NYC to be checked out and see what new chemotherapy they have on their menu du jour. My oncologist is not anxious to have me get caught up in a chemo plan that causes more damage than good. I have known since the beginning that this cancer was a bad one and my chances were not good. Chemotherapy seems to maybe add sixty or ninety days, but it could be at a terrible cost and might just plain not be worth it. Having said that, I am meeting with the head of the St. Francis Cancer Center for a review of my case that will include evaluations for chemotherapy, but again, this is for potential treatment and only if a real benefit with minimal side effects is predicted.

The doctors don't like predicting, but six to twelve months keeps coming up in conversation. I am ready for whatever happens. I am not stressed, and I sleep like a baby. I have told you that my Lord and Savior is with me, and that has not changed. My prayers are now for Cindy, that she have the strength to handle this stuff and continue with her own life. She is my best friend.

Kathy and Kurt, a niece and nephew of mine, came up for a short visit on Saturday. They stopped at Lino's Market here in Durham and brought enough lunch that we will be eating it for a week. They also brought the largest, richest chocolate cake I have ever seen, straight from one of Kurt's favorite restaurants back in New Jersey. Thank you, guys.

Lots of people have been stopping in. Last weekend, it was Chris, Karen, Neil, Luke, and Michael, my brother's children and grandchildren. It is always nice to visit with relatives you don't see often enough. I hope to make a swing down to New Jersey to see as many as possible before winter sets in and restricts our driving.

I am tired almost all the time and need to sit down. I can stand and walk a bit, but it is a chore. Sitting, I am good for three or four hours and then need to lie down for a while to relax the chest muscles that seem to bunch up lately.

WRITTEN OCTOBER 24, 2011, 10:25 P.M.

This is a confusing time for me right now. I have had two similar lung operations. After the first, I had numbness in one section of my chest and a pain way in front. The doctor went into my chest through my armpit and then a little farther around the back right side. The numbness and pain subsided, and I did well with it for five months. Then the shortness of breath brought on the CT scans and the rather hurried surgery to "weld" my plural sacks together. Now I have a distinct pain in the right side of my chest, a nagging cough, and local pain at the incision sites. The problem is that I don't know whether I will be getting any better from the second operation ... or if this is this the best to expect until further symptoms develop. No one can answer that question for me. Oh, yes, and my A-fib still makes any activity a chore. Having said all of that, I am not complaining. I am merely stating that I wish I knew more about what to expect as far as healing from my operation goes. I think the doctors don't have the faintest idea either.

Thank you to all those who read my blog, and a special thanks to those of you who have passed on words of encouragement or were impacted by something I wrote. The blog has taken on a life of its own. I visit it frequently just to see if someone wrote, and I enjoy all of the feedback. I am kind of amazed that I am writing such a chronicle as I have never seen anything like this, nor was I particularly excited about it when my daughter, Erica, suggested it. I can only say that the blog has done wonders keeping all of my friends and relatives on the same page while minimizing the phone calls. It is very seldom that I need to explain to anyone "how I'm doing."

You might think that the information about my sickness is pretty personal and difficult to share. That could not be further from the truth. I feel as if I have worth during these last months to show you what terminal cancer looks like from the perspective of a friend going through it. With God's help, death has no grip on me. My copilot still sits with me, and I believe He will continue to do so as long as I ask Him to stay. I am living a miracle every day, and I hope that you can see that. There is time for all of you to ask God's blessing on the remainder of your lives. Remember that Jesus forgave the thief on the cross literally minutes before he died. All the thief had to do was acknowledge Jesus as his Lord and Savior and ask forgiveness. If you are overwhelmed by where I am, I can understand that. Everyone needs to start easy with the truth and work their way into understanding the word of God. I urge you to purchase a book titled *A Case for Christ* written by Lee Strobel. Take the time to read the book carefully. Read it with an open mind, challenge all of it, but read it. It may have everlasting implications on your life.

Thank you for your friendship. Thank you for your encouragement. Thank you for reading and commenting in our blog.

Written October 27, 2011, 12:22 a.m.

So how did I get to this point?

Born in 1946 to two German immigrant parents, Herman and Helen Schwiindeler, I was the youngest of three boys, followed by my sister, who came ten years later. My father emigrated to New York City in 1928 and returned to his brother's wedding in German in 1930 only to meet his brother's wife's sister and fall in love. So two Schwiindeler brothers married two Hempen sisters. My cousins are double first cousins and look more like my brothers than cousins.

At eighteen years old, my mother chose to leave her family and travel to America with this tall, red-haired man just a few months after she had met him. Her family was devastated by her departure. They were married by both a priest and a justice in order to get all the paperwork needed for emigration.

What about the name change? So our family name is Schwiindeler, which is an honorable name in Germany but not a great name to have in the United States. My dad requested permission from his dad to change the name to Schulte, a name that many of the men in the family were called in Germany as it denoted that they were the mayor of their small town of Hasselunne. *Schulte* means mayor in German.

Once in New Jersey, my mom was desperately lonely for a while but began to fit in when my brother Frank came along. My mom was an amazing woman who had four "only" children. My brother Frank was born in 1932 and will be eighty next year. My brother Joe was born six years later in 1938. I was born in 1946, and my sister, Annmarie, was born in 1956. My mother spaced her four kids out over twenty-four years.

She was a stay-at-home mom, something my father was very proud about and something that I will always be thankful for.

I had several uncles who fought in WWII (on the German side) and who lost their lives. It was a difficult time to be of German descent in America, especially because my dad was president of the German Club in Bloomfield, NJ. Our home was visited by government officials more than once during and even after the war. I think it wasn't until my brother Frank entered the military (on our side) that the visits stopped.

I was born in 1946! I was the postwar baby, soon to be labeled a "baby boomer." I had an idyllic childhood. We had no TV. We played outside until the streetlights came on. We wore out bicycle tires, wore spring clips to keep the pant cuffs out of the chains, and put baseball cards in the spokes with clothes pins to make a cool noise. We rode on bicycle handlebars, in the back of open pickup trucks, and in the rumble seats of some of the older roadsters that were still on the road. Seat belts were for jet pilots. We had BB guns, hunted rats in the dump, and walked everywhere. We had no cell phones. Heck, when I picked up our black phone, someone on the other end said, "Number please?" By the way, my home phone number was "Bloomfield 2-4297M" and was spoken just that way to the operator. We had a four-party line, but that's a whole other story. As kids, we were always looking to find money. We collected bottles for their deposit, coat hangers to sell back to the cleaners for a penny each, and newspapers to sell to the rag man when his horse and wagon came around the neighborhood. We wanted to earn money to fund our "Black Cat Club." I found our paperwork this week. The club was officially closed and the money divided on June 8, 1960. I was a member of this club from about nine until thirteen years old.

My dad was a partner in a hardware store that struggled along for my entire childhood. I helped out by helping him sharpen and repair lawnmowers, saws, and knives. I can still remember taking the annual inventory using a "Burroughs" adding machine that had a million push-down numbers on the front and a long handle on the right side that you pulled on to enter the number just keyed in. If you had ten of an item, you keyed in the item cost, held down the "repeat" key, and pulled the handle ten times!

My brother Frank was fourteen years older than me, and by the time I got to high school, he was already twenty-seven years old and owned a small carpentry business. My father had apprenticed him to an old Italian carpenter named Dave Montini, who taught him the trade and then sold his business to him. Dave had an old 1950 Chevy truck with the famed "blue flame" in-line six-cylinder engine that no one could wear out. It went with the business. I worked for Frank all summer long while in high school, and he paid me two dollars per day and five dollars for Saturdays. Yup, fifteen dollars per week, and believe me, we worked. No one had air-conditioning back then. He was a big guy—six-foot-three and maybe a solid 255 pounds. I was almost as tall by then but a skinny 150 pounds, and there were times when no one other than Frank could do a particular part of the job we were working on. One job, I recall, was hot tar roofing. I tended the kettle on the ground. I chopped up the blocks of tar and melted them down, while Frank used the fiberglass mop, which weighed about forty pounds, to spread the heavy tar over the paper we laid down. It was hard work, but it was worth it to be able to brag about it now. Frank taught me to shoot, and we hunted together. We were both members of a gun club and shot trap on club property in Northern New Jersey. I spent a lot of time with Frank, but I had a special love for my father, who died on my eighteenth birthday.

More later.

Written October 28, 2011, 10:37 p.m.

I breezed right over my early education yesterday, so let's go back to 1951 when my folks enrolled me into Sacred Heart School, the same school that educated both of my brothers and would eventually have my sister as a student. We were a member family at Sacred Heart Catholic Church, and "our pew" was on the main aisle, specifically the second row on the left side. That was our pew, and nobody else sat there in the eight o'clock service. From there, we could gaze right into the eyes of Monsignor Burke while he gave us his sermon each Sunday.

School was taught by the Sisters of Charity, and I have many fond memories of my elementary years. Our close connection to the church, my father owning the hardware store, and my brother being the school carpenter really cemented our relationship, and I had a wonderful primary school experience. Frank's shop was on the school grounds, and I was quite the celebrity to be able to stop in to see him when the shop was occupied. I shall always remember the glowing potbelly stove on the cold winter days. My brother Joe was eight years older than me, so he was in a different league of friends than I was, and I rarely interacted with him. He played football for Immaculate Conception High School and married a cute blonde cheerleader. Joan and Joe are still together after all of these years.

In 1960, I went on to Essex Catholic High School in Newark, NJ. We were taught by the Irish Christian Brothers, who had the nickname of International Child Beaters. There was no lack of corporal punishment in those days, and several times, I had to touch my toes while I accepted a few shots from a shoe leather strap across my backside. I survived, as did all the other kids, and we actually thrived in the relationships that we forged both with teachers and other students. In my thirteen years of Catholic schooling, I never experienced or witnessed any of the things that brought so many priests down over the past twenty years.

My dad had his first stroke just about the time I went off to high school, and my mom had to get her first job (something that greatly troubled my dad). He so wanted to take care of all of us on his own. My parents were peasant stock. They both finished only eight years of school in Germany. They raised four kids, and I don't think any of us ever realized that we really didn't have any real money.

Everything was hand-to-mouth and odd jobs or after school, and summer work was normal.

After high school, I worked for the New Jersey Bell Telephone Co. and attended Fairleigh Dickinson University at night. I held the following positions over the four years that I worked for Bell: frameman in Bellville, NJ, installer in Montclair, NJ, and repair service in Newark, NJ. By far my favorite job ever was installation in Montclair. I was assigned a truck, and each morning, I got a fistful of orders, picked up the phones I needed, and headed out for the day. It was a new freedom for me, and I was a natural at it. My dad was proud that I worked for a public utility. He had his second stroke on my birthday and died three days later in 1965.

His death was the first one that close to me. I can vividly remember waking up on the day after his death in disbelief that the world could possibly go on and that I would have to continue without him. My mom died many years later at the age of eighty-nine. I will always be indebted to both my parents for preparing me to deal with whatever life sent my way.

WRITTEN NOVEMBER 1, 2011, 5:37 P.M.

The past few days have not been good. I am starving for air and having difficulty sleeping.

Today's doctor's appointment resulted in my being enrolled in the Connecticut Hospice Program out of Branford.

Things will be speeding up now. Lots of thoughts about things to do and preparations to make. There is not much time left.

WRITTEN NOVEMBER 2, 2011, 6:35 P.M.

Short update: Hospice changed to Middletown at our request. First in house and then in hospital as needed.

Doubled the oxygen and using a breathing machine about eighteen hours per day. We are still at my in-laws in Haddam but hope to get home by Friday. My son, Adam, is flying in tomorrow morning. I want to get to church on Sunday, but it is really iffy. I need a wheelchair at the very least.

Everyone is taking great care of me. (I have zero energy.) And I am blessed by my family and friends. I have no fear. The Devil must be really pissed off about now. Jesus is still sitting next to me and shares His comfort with me. I would not trade my place with anyone in the world. I am now praying for you. I pray that you come to the realization that life is only a short stop off on our way to paradise. I pray that my openness smacks you upside the head and gets your attention. This is the way to go out, with Jesus at your side. I am honored by His presence. You can have it too.

WRITTEN NOVEMBER 3, 2011, 4:28 P.M.

Your comments today brought me to tears, not tears of sorrow but of joy! It is clear to me that I am being heard, and I will continue to pray for you all.

My head is still screwed on tight; however, the morphine begins tomorrow, and I expect to get a little dull around the edges. I promise to continue to write until I can no longer do it. I trust you will excuse my writing if it rambles or doesn't sound like me.

I just want to get something out while I am clear. My life has been blessed in so many ways, and the affection that I feel from all of you is awesome. Please know that we were truly friends and that I care about how you live your lives and deal with adversity. God has been my answer, and I am "all in" with Him. When I surrendered "me" to Him, I found myself in Him, and He will not let me down. I so want for all of us to be linked by the same "best friend," Jesus Christ.

So I don't know how I will sound from here on in, but I think you know me now. It has been my pleasure to know each of you in my life, and it is a very special experience for me to be a part of Fellowship Church at a time when God was performing so many miracles and showing us the way He wanted it done. I am so grateful to Pastor Andy for helping me realize that the best way forward was to let God lead and follow Him. It has been an E ticket ride.

With great love and affection,
Captain Bob

AMAZING GRACE

WRITTEN NOVEMBER 6, 2011, 6:01 A.M.

It is early, early Sunday morning. Guess whose internal clock is still on the other time? I started a journal entry last night, but after I came close to completing it, I lost it to the great Toshiba Devil and had to do it over. It seems as if I have a lot to tell you.

First, let me say that my son, Adam, who lives in Medford, Oregon, arrived safely on Thursday, and he has been a workhorse for us since then. I am so proud to have him as a son. Loaned him my car, as I can't drive on these meds until we see how I handle them, and he saw that the oil change light is on, so *voila*, oil change done, and I am all set. Restock refrigerator—check. Ice cream—check. Two kinds of ice cream—check. (Oh, did I ever mention that since I got the Hospice party invite, I decided that there would be a whole lot more hot fudge Sundays in my future?) He cooked a great, I mean restaurant-quality corn chowder for last night's supper—check. Oh, by the way, he cooked up three gallons and froze off portions—check. If you stop by in the next three weeks or so, you have a chance for a cup of the best!

Adam will be headed back to Oregon after first service today. (Thank you, Debbie, for driving him to the airport.) I am sure I will be a basket case. Love does that.

Now on to the partial results on the medications that I am now using. It has been just one full day, but I am astounded by the efficacy of these drugs. I caution you to understand that they are only masking symptoms, not curing anything, but they make me feel human again. I can deeply breathe and walk longer distances, and even my heart seems to be beating in sync again. I am cautioned to not overdo it, so I will still be seen with oxygen bottle in tow and using a wheelchair; however, the difference between Friday and now is very significant. My quality of life just got a whole lot better. Thank you, Jesus.

Now for a rundown on the new medicine protocol. First, I am wearing some sort of morphine patch. It is very small (size of a quarter), and the dosage is very light. Each patch will last for three days before we replace it with another on an appointed hour. The dosage is administered very slowly and at a constant rate, almost as if I had a personal IV dragging at my side. Morphine is a pain med and has completely erased the pain that I had across my chest. It also suppresses my autonomic function to gasp for air when my oxygen saturation drops below 90 percent. I am taking longer, deeper breathes on my own without the constant panting or coughing that was driving me a little crazy these past two weeks.

Second, I am taking a steroid in pill form twice a day. The steroid will reduce the inflammation that surrounds the cancer itself, which lives on the chest wall separating my lungs and heart. The reduction reduces the irritation and further reduces the cough factor—nice.

Third, I have available to me an "as needed" Xanax-type drug to take the edges off if I become upset or irritated. I can take half to one pill as needed. I tried one whole pill in the safety of my own home yesterday morning, and it was a little stronger than I expected. It was calming but a bit more than needed. It tired me out. I won't be using that drug again unless I need the cavalry.

Fourth, I have a big bottle of morphine, my very own "stash." It is for breakthrough pain and is used "as needed." I just squirt a little between my cheek and gum and wash it down with some OJ. It is remarkably powerful stuff and needs respect.

I cannot say enough about the whole hospice approach. Flat out, they live to make me comfortable. I have a "worldly" advocate group to ease my way to heaven. I am overwhelmed by their sincerity and professionalism, perhaps even more so by their ability to answer my questions and tell me almost exactly how these drugs will coincide with each other.

I feel that I am in very good hands all around. My wife is here, and we are able to enjoy our time together. The hospice nurses are solving my symptom issues, and my God is holding my hand as we walk down this final earthy path. Honestly, can you come up with a better scenario than that? I have so much to be thankful for right now. I have said it before, and I'll say it again: I would not trade places with any other living man right now. I can see the light of heaven ahead, and I will stay focused on that light and direction.

A Prayer for Us All

Heavenly Father, Lord of lords, Jesus, I thank you for how You are still serving me today. That You would suffer on the cross to forgive my sins even before I was born, that you would inspire the writers of the Bible to create a roadmap for me to use in life, that you would answer my prayers and bless me with grace, as I gift You with my faith, that You would create a heavenly home for me to come to when I am done is beyond normal comprehension. Thank you, Jesus, for allowing me to understand what is happening to me right now so that I am witness to Your eternal power. Thank you, Jesus, for bringing all of these blog readers together to witness my love letters to You, and thank you, Jesus, for each person who becomes thirsty for Your love through my writing so that I may enjoy their company in paradise when they are saved. Thank you for my children and my grandchildren, and may they grow closer and closer to You over time. Thank you for saving me at age fifty-five, as I did nothing to deserve Your love … but that is the point. It was freely given on the cross, and we must understand we can do nothing to deserve it. We must just accept it. Thank you, thank you. Amen.

PS: See you in Fellowship Church at 9:30 today!

MY NEW CHEMISTRY SET

WRITTEN NOVEMBER 7, 2011, 7:14 A.M.

Well, my son, Adam, left for Medford, Oregon, yesterday right after church and right after a very emotional farewell. Thank you, Adam, that we could cry openly and say the words that needed said. Adam and I have not had a great record for communication. We both want to clean that up and got off to an honest start. Thank you, Jesus. Prayers answered.

Unfortunately, Adam is stuck in Cleveland of all places until about 5:00 p.m. tonight. Continental Airlines oversold his flight, and he was not issued a boarding pass in Cleveland. The airline will pay for his hotel, dinner, breakfast, and lunch plus some sort of voucher. Unfortunately, Adam will have to use a vacation day to make up for money lost. Irritating!

I am just a couple of days into the hospice program and am very encouraged. I have a team working on keeping me as comfortable as possible with meds that really do work. It is a little confusing for the newbie as I need to master the mixes of drugs that seem to work best. Cindy is my official caregiver and has serious responsibility for helping me understand and use these drugs. She is tracking every dose level and time taken for review with our nurse supervisor. I can see where it will take some time to get the hang of it, and I can begin to understand why I will not be left alone during the hospice program. We have already had to "hire a babysitter for me" for later this week while Cindy gets to go to the airport to pick our daughter, Beth, who is flying in from Austin, TX.

This morning when I awoke, I had a little pressure on my chest and a shortness of breath. I needed my regular morning pills but also had to take my earliest dose of morphine yet for relief. It is much better after twenty minutes, but new stuff is scary when first encountered. Nurse C, who is my key communicator right now, is available 24-7 in person or by phone. That is a wonderful insurance policy. I am sure we will be spending many hours in consultation as we learn how to best manage this changing situation. It is strange to know that we are purposefully trying to mask the bad stuff going on. All of my past medical activity has been with all eyes toward healing. Now all eyes are toward hiding.

WRITTEN NOVEMBER 8, 2011, 8:21 P.M.

Had a busy day today. Started out with Bennett and Sadie coming over to spend the day with their grandparents as the Middletown School System was closed for Election Day activities in the school polling places. Having been a registrar, I can tell you that everything from parking to polling place layout can get really confusing when school is open as well.

My big softy brother Frank and his wife, Gerda, drove all the way up again from New Jersey to see us, and they brought Italian sandwiches with them from Lino's, our favorite local store. They are such a great couple, and I am so happy they found each other after both of their longtime partners died over ten years ago. The match was made in heaven for Frank and Gerda. As a matter of fact, I think Gerda may be an angel as that is probably what it will take to keep my brother in line.

We had a great time together, and I must say that knowing the end is near makes saying the important things so much easier. I can look people in the eye and mean and say, "I love you," and they don't weird out on me. The clarity I am enjoying right now is incredible. I feel like I have my life under a magnifying glass, and for the first time, I am understanding relationships that have completely mixed me up prior to this. God sure is great at straightening this stuff out. He still sits next to me and maybe even inspires a key or two on this typewriter. (Oops, am I dating myself by saying typewriter?) My professional career started in 1968, and I can assure you that the very best machine around was the IBM Selectric. It could type through four carbon pages at a time, and the Wite-Out came in gallon jugs.

Today was more chemistry. I mentioned healing v. hiding when we use medications. Most of us take a medication, and if we feel better, we act better with more pep and energy. That is not so in hospice. The better you feel, the better you are masking a symptom and the more careful you have to be to not overdo it because you feel better. Push yourself too far because you feel better, and you could fall into a trap and have to redo all the medications to balance things off again.

Today, I learned that my fentanyl patch was too weak for me, and I was using lots of morphine to catch up. The answer to that was to double the strength of the fentanyl and watch closely again as we see how much morphine I use for breakthrough pain. By the way, the breakthrough pain I have is really not painful, just nagging. I have been told that I have a high threshold for pain, so I have to be proactive in taking meds before it gets any worse. Once you miss the magic time to treat for pain, it is possible to lose control, and then you chance having the pain for a couple of days before you get it under control again. That happened once to me when I had the original surgery on my left leg, and I can assure you that that was no fun.

Anyway, once you get the pain handled, then the heart and lungs have to agree to breathe deeply and use the oxygen provided. Well, I have a bad right lung, probably putting out 50 percent or less than desired, and an as yet unaffected left lung. We use sedative-type drugs to suppress the brain's becoming hyperactive and causing panting, which is no fun. We also use steroids to reduce the inflammation around the cancer tumors themselves.

So it all becomes a Cirque du Soleil balancing act. Trick the body with drugs to keep the breathing coming, while you wait for the other shoe to drop somewhere. I am learning a lot and enjoying the many visits from friends and relatives. I use Google Calendar to keep track of the visitations, and it seems to be doing well. I feel good still and enjoy visiting and sharing my testimony. Here is a shout-out to my double first cousin in North Carolina: Hubert and Linda, come on up, call me, don't come up just for me, but I would love to see you guys.

Cindy and I got to vote tonight. I was able to get that darn wheelchair out of Cindy's car and wheel myself all around, visiting with poll workers as we voted in our municipal elections. I pray that my candidates get in as they have done excellent jobs these past four years.

I have had some meaningful conversations these past few days. I hope they continue. God bless you for reading and praying along with me. I am telling everyone that the surrender prayer, where you give it all to Christ, is the one that brought Him into my sickroom permanently. If you need Jesus, He is over here at my house.

WRITTEN NOVEMBER 10, 2011, 6:20 A.M.

The past twenty-four hours have been good. We had a minor failure with the "patch" delivery system, which gives me meds through a patch on my back. The membrane was dried out in one package, so I had to administer more meds orally to make up for the loss. Easily done as when the patch stopped working, the pain level in my chest told me something was wrong, I just compensated after a quick call to the 24-7 hospice nurse. She later came over and changed systems.

We had many visitors yesterday and had great times all around. It is fun to stare with wonder into each others eyes as God revealed His power and planning. I must begin to sound like an old record on some of this stuff, but I am still blown away daily by my personal contact with Jesus and His care for me.

I apologize to some of you who have asked to visit. I have had to resort to Google Calendar to keep track, and I leave a little rest time in between. It seems to be working out. Some of you are bringing food, and that works too; however, I hate to just have you do that without a visit. But if the house is full or I am resting, that's the best I can do. Bennett asked me if I was going to be here for Christmas, so I now have a goal if the Lord wills it. We have tickets again for the Christmas North Pole Train down in Essex, but I don't think I will be up for such a strenuous evening activity. I guess I will send the rest of the family with video cameras and hope to get into that special evening's spirit that way. We will see. Maybe.

I have had to drop out of my men's Bible study, just because I must conserve strength. I am going to ask if Rich Pancoast, our group leader, might allow me to address the guys through him each week on the thoughts I had relative to the Sunday service.

I hope to be able to get to church as regularly as possible on Sundays. I have to be smart about it, but I can't think of a nicer place to be if the time comes. It is important that *no one call 911* if the end comes then. I am on a DNR/DNI (Do not resuscitate/Do not intubate) program with hospice, so special transport or none at all is in order rather than the 911 drill. I hope that this is not too disruptive if it plays out that way. An impromptu hymn and send-me-off to heaven—that would be neat. What a way to go.

TINY THOUGHTS OF DEATH

WRITTEN NOVEMBER 11, 2011, 5:35 A.M.

I guess I can't help it. Sometimes I just think about death, about how it will steal into the room and take me. I feel remarkably well with perhaps just a little vertigo thrown in. I exit my hospital bed to starboard and list that way, trying to standup straight. I have to go back to using a cane nearby or maybe even a walker to hang onto when I first rise. My walker is heavy. I would like to borrow one with two wheels on it so that I can easily push it along in front of me on the first trip to the head in the morning.

I think I ate too much last night after we got back from buying Cindy her new "Arrest Me Red" Subaru Forester. I had turkey and homemade cranberry sauce followed by cookies, ice cream, and Foxon soda (the best local soda around). I had to ask Cindy to sit with me for a while as I was having strange feeling across my chest. I had also been off my oxygen for too long. The feeling cleared up, and it was just a nice, quiet, short visit that Cindy and I shared before I dropped off to sleep. She has the tough job now. I ask that you pray not for me but for Cindy. She is faced with having to be the real big-time survivor here. She is strong but has the same human fears any of us experience. My witnessing makes it easy for her to see why I want to go, but that doesn't make it any easier for her to say good-bye. We are taking the time necessary to let tears flow, but it is really painful. I cannot explain to you how gracious, loving, and thoughtful Cindy has been to me for my whole marriage, much less the year and eight months we have been fighting this cancer actively. Again, your prayers are so appreciated for her. Please pray specifically that her family crowd around her and create a hedge of protection for her from the world for a time and from the Devil forever. We believe in "spiritual warfare" in my family, and the Devil tries people when they are weakest. Cindy's faith is superb, but the Devil pecking at her footsteps would be a pain. Just pray that the demons be gone in the name of God the Father and that He provide her with the peace that passes all understanding, the peace that only God can provide.

The hospice folks have been so nice. My family is so spread out—Oregon, Minnesota, Texas, and thankfully Middletown. Our one wish is that perhaps we get a couple of days indication that the end is near so that several of us may be together with Cindy at the end.

Remember to say your prayers. Remember that time is short. Remember to tell the one you love that you love them. Start with Jesus.

Chapter 9

I Have No Fear

For the last few weeks, I have been a spectator on a long, gentle ride toward heaven.

Now there is a change. Jesus, my best friend, is now alongside me, answering prayers of mine that are years old. He has not forgotten them. I am become much more than a spectator now. It is almost as if Jesus is showing His power one more time for me so that I, a lowly Bob Schulte, may get to see Him from the box seats. Oh, His miracles started with the big things. He took all my fear and turned it into wonder! I could not believe that He wanted to carry me through this sickness the way He was. I was and continue to be all gratitude for that. I have no fear. *I have no fear!*

It is now the small stuff that is making the difference, He has not forgotten the small prayers that I prayed at Fellowship with the prayer team. Many of our praying men will remember me praying for my children, that they are drawn closer to Him over time, find happiness, forgiveness, God, and love before too long. Many have heard me pray for a better relationship with Adam, Beth, even Rich, and my grandchildren. Now God is bringing up the old prayers, the ones where I pray for my sister and her relationship with kids, husband, and especially we three older brothers, Frank, Joe, and Bob. Our family once was very close, due in part to the strong character of two women, Helen, my mom, and Margaret, my brother's widow. Those two kept the brother's talking, the sister admiring, and the world at bay. They called for family gatherings by telling you what to bring, not by asking if you could make it. It was a wonderful matrilineal group that we were members of. God bless our women.

Only after they both left us did we fall into the habit of poor communication and perhaps insincere talk at that. Our individual families took up our time, and we were in the midst of life's frenzy. All the usual sicknesses, graduations, births, business failures, and general busyness just caused us to rust on the outside and grow cold on the in.

God has reopened a window to the past for us all. He has remembered my prayers and perhaps my siblings' prayers at this time. All of the brothers and my sister as well have had a chance to stick their necks out and look back into the window, to take a look around, to wonder if we may once again share as we did, love as we did, communicate that love as we did. I have been blessed because I cleared all of the air I needed to for me. My brothers and sister know how much I love them. I have cried with and for each of them. Yesterday in my home, my sister and her entire family cried with me, not for my pending death but for the renewal that we may find in our relationships shown now in the full glory of the Son of Man. We spoke of the job futures for one, sports and travel teams for another, schooling for yet another, and long-term happiness in a family for a lovely woman thinking about sharing her life with we Steimle/Schultes. God is allowing us to voice our prayers out loud to each other again. I pray that we all listen and answer each other again as we did when we were younger. I have a great family. Thank you, Jesus, for reminding me. Thank you for opening the party again.

WRITTEN NOVEMBER 14, 2011, 5:16 A.M.

Life continues as it has done for me for sixty-five years now, but there is a growing noise as I become sensitive to a finish line of sorts. While, on the one hand, the favors of my Lord are raining down on me spiritually in a continuous pitter-patter of blessings, on the other, my friends and relatives pull so hard to make me wish to stay. My Lord's invitation has been accepted, and I love my friends so much for their loyalty and effort to comfort my transition.

Yesterday turned out to be one of the best days of my life for so many reasons. Let me try to scratch the surface for you. First, a dear friend from town decided to come to church with me for the first time. She pulled up a chair next to my wheelchair and enjoyed the praise and worship we offer God each week. If all you want to do is grow the kingdom of God, you know how thrilled I was to have her there. Later on in the evening, her whole family visited our home, and we spoke of important things, things like salvation, children making choices, and how our family could be a blessing to her as job opportunities, career choices, and just good living present themselves to her two kids, Sam and Sara. Two of the greatest kids (besides my own) I have ever known. I hope that Cindy and they remain close. Cindy would benefit from the "checking in on" every now and again.

Yesterday, we had our founding pastor speak to us. He and Sandy now live in South Carolina, but they visited home to say hello to their children and grandchildren who live up this way. Pastor Steve always has the opportunity to address his old congregation when he travels this way. There was a time when Steve and I could name every person in the congregation. That is no longer true now as God has been building on Steve's hard work and Andy (Steve's son) now is our senior pastor. Andy's "Seeker Sunday" approach to ministry has made it easy for people to find us on the Internet, drive by our church, or just hear about us from our members. The chairs have been filled twice again now, and we are meeting some of the greatest sinners I know to worship and seek growth in spiritual lives. Oh, if it wasn't for the sinners, our church would be empty. I like it full of real people taking honest steps and doing it along with me.

We had an early Christmas party yesterday for staff workers, ministry leaders, and their families. The food was great—fruit, hot pasta with shrimp, salads, cookies, drinks, all the stuff that church people are famous for. We had the extra benefit of having our own famous "Chef Amy," who has a short TV program, a saucy personality, and great ideas for new recipes. She and her extended family are all members of Fellowship and bring color to our Sundays. Thank you, Amy.

The party included a time for reminiscence. Two of our oldest members, Barbara and Richard, have sold their house and are moving down to Fellowship South (South Carolina where our senior pastor lives). Several of our families have retired down that way, and we all wish them great happiness and fellowship as they complete their own journeys through live together.

The party also became an emotional time for me, as we together addressed my sickness openly. Many projects and activities that I have worked on within the church were highlighted, and in perhaps the most difficult segment, I was presented with at least seventy cards and letters from the LP (Living Proof) Youth Group members thanking me for things that they appreciated about one or another job that I had worked on. Here I am at 4:27 a.m. in the morning, and the tears freely flow. I had no idea that what I was doing could affect these students and leaders as it has. I sit in shock that my life could be considered important. I pray that I contain my ego and not allow this most open of demonstrations of love to go to my head.

Lord, thank you for the opportunity to serve. Thank you for making it so easy to serve so that I didn't feel like a hero. Thank you for the generosity of these students words, and thank you for finishing the LP room on time for these great people to have a safe place to come on Friday nights. Thank you that they cared to say thanks and that they shared some of the inner battles that they already wage against the evil one with the help of Your council. Amen.

I got a call from my friend Paul and his wife, Sandy. They are flying in from California to see me. No question, just a statement: We're coming." I have known Paul for over sixty years. He lived on the same block as me. We played every day after school, had our Black Cat Club, and explored incessantly by walking, biking, or just running through the park. I went to his pool, and he visited me at Lake Shawnee, where we had a small cabin with relatives. We tried a "lean-to" in the back woods and scared the daylights out of ourselves. I don't remember my life without "Paulie." I love him so much. Thank you, Paul, for what you mean to me. I am sure it wasn't easy for our two families to accept each other as they did. Paul was my best friend by 1950, though his name was Konwiser, a fine Jewish name, and mine was Schulte, a fine German name, not to mention that my father was the president of the German Club right through WWII. Many thought it strange that two families just dealing with the reality of the Holocaust could allow their children to become such friends. Sally and Walter Konwiser were saints to me, and they have long held that status. I never remember even one instance of prejudice. I hope my family did as well for Paul. Thank you, Ma and Pa Konwiser as well as Ma and Pa Schulte.

WRITTEN NOVEMBER 15, 2011, 9:33 P.M.

My life has been very confusing since my doctors made the hospice decision with me and the family. God has been doing so many good things for me, and yet I didn't seem to be able to pass them along in a believable manner to you. I seemed to have something too good to be true to sing about; however, I could not explain myself to you, and even worse, I was having a difficult time thanking God directly for His ministrations to me. I was at a loss for words for you and for Him. It reminded me of a sales program I once had to sell for Stanley Tools. It was a completely honest program with guaranteed sales, long dating (payback time) free freight, free displays, and in-store service. The problem was that there was almost no cost to the dealer, and he could not bring himself around to believing that he could get such a good deal. There had to be hidden costs. The dealer couldn't recognize that Stanley needed them so badly to display the merchandise that the first issues of merchandise could be sacrificed in order to get the pipeline filled for secondary orders. The Stanley Preview Dealer Program subsequently became one of the strongest sales events we ever had, and we brought out four different flights of product under the program each year for many years. I made great strides forward in my career with Stanley by selling the heck out of that unique program. Finally, dealers began to believe in it, and then it was like shooting ducks in a pond. They loved it.

So here I am in the grip of Jesus Christ, being carried right through this ending period of my life, and I am again struggling to tell people about it. I am still tongue-tied, frustrated with my words, and unconvincing because it is too good a deal. People think me crazy as opposed to saved.

Most of you know me as I know most of you. I am telling the truth. You, too, may have Jesus in your heart, holding you up and carrying you to heaven. Pray for His forgiveness, pray for His understanding, and finally pray for the Holy Spirit to help you tell Jesus how appreciative you are for His gift of grace. I think I will have some interesting information about that in a future blog.

Prayer

God, hear me through my helpmate, the Holy Spirit, as I try to tell you what an impact you are having on my life. I am amazed that you would love me enough to share heaven with me. I deserve none of your freely given grace. I am a sinner among sinners, not even a man among men. Thank you for letting me see the beauty of your home, hear the music of the angels, and witness the seasons of God.

WRITTEN NOVEMBER 16, 2011, 1:23 A.M.

My friends, it is getting harder to do everything. I scare myself because of my early morning and evening stumbling. Tears of losing you all fill my day. I think I said what I had to say about salvation, and I know that I am getting through to people who care. I need to take some time off. I am cutting back on my visiting hours. I am down about thirty pounds, and pretty soon, I will have a six-pack like Rich's. I want to try to extend now. I have a Christmas date to try to make. Please pray that I make that date. I love you all. My blog will be shorter now. Your prayers right there in the guestbook area would be greatly appreciated. It is your blog now.

SOME RELIEF

WRITTEN NOVEMBER 18, 2011, 6:18 A.M.

These last few days have been extremely difficult, but I am still sore, sticking myself with needles, mentally confused and stumbling around, so I must be on earth.

My body flew out of shape chemically with my Coumadin level running up to over ten when it should be near two. They were worried I would start to hemorrhage from one end to the other. Then my sugar level made me crazy, running up to 572, many times above what is normal. The sugar ride was no fun as my grandkids were here and I scared not only myself but my family. I could not speak straight, and a sentence might start out speaking of school and end up somewhere else talking about motor mechanics. *Thank you, God, that my older grandkids were here and that we somehow managed to turn it into a sick joke. It was no fun!*

Mack, call out!

Mack, I remember how great you are, and I thank God that you allowed me to say a few things that helped me years ago when I had a breakup. There is no accounting for changes in the wind. People change as they grow. I am a better person because of my first breakup, and so is she. It took the basting, baking, resting, and growing in our lives to show us that in greater maturity, we were not the people who fell in love earlier. We turned out wiser, more mature, closer to God, maybe even better people, but "not the people who fell in love earlier." Captain Bob says, "Grow tall and prosper." You are so fortunate to have been loved as you are for who you are and by many. So many will never feel the pain of love that you feel now. That is a terrible shame. *Live on, cowgirl!*

Prayer

Dear God, Father of us all, thank you for pain. Thank you for the contrast that we may apply to happiness so we may rejoice in it with you. Thank you for the colors and the rains and the snows so we may experience life here. Without these primer steps, heaven might overpower us as you lead us home. Bless the saddened, love the unloved. Cause each of us to *stop* and look around for someone else to help. Bring us to church faithfully to witness your miracles working around us. Find no blame for growth in life. Lead us as sheep to your forage land and gather us together for the final never-ending feast that we will enjoy with the Trinity in Heaven. Amen.

Written November 20, 2011, 6:02 p.m.

We have been pretty busy up here in Connecticut. I was admitted to the Middlesex Hospital Hospice Unit at about 10:00 p.m. Saturday night and have been there ever since. Sorry I missed church. My chemical balance was all out of shape. My sugar numbers jumped from normal to almost six hundred points because of the steroids that I was on for the cancer. I was incoherent for at least two full days. Having said that, some people thought I was more normal.

The doctors hope to get me home for Thanksgiving, and lots of family decisions are being made. As I can let you know what is going on, I will, but privacy and quality family time is becoming more important to us all. We appreciate so much all of the time, food, visitations, and well-wishes that we have seen from you. We have asked Vicki to coordinate friends and family who would like to drop off a meal for us in the future. Once we have settled in back home, we will try to come up with a better way to handle visits as well.

WRITTEN NOVEMBER 21, 2011, 6:32 A.M.

The first notice of day was Barbara asking me when my birthday was. She then slide the little needle into my arm, and the real day began. PT-INR test for blood thinner. No biggie that one, just a pinch.

Today, we are moving into a new, longer-acting insulin (Lantus?) that should slow this up-and-down cycle we seem caught in. I would like to feel normal for a day. Hey, maybe a new TV show titled *Normal for a Day.*

I find that I am a social butterfly enjoying conversation with the wonderful staff here. There is less opportunity for me to interact with "residents." They are people who are dealing with their own demons, trying to get used to their new situation. I haven't figured out how I might actively help, but I intend to put my "prayer warrior" status on the line and talk to Jesus about them, At night, I can hear gentle weeping coming from one room. I will concentrate there first.

Even though I am super excited about going home to my precious Savior, I/we (Cindy and I) weep on a moment's notice. Erica and her children, Cole and Lara, had to return to Minneapolis and are in the sky right now. I don't know why it hadn't dawned on us, but when they were saying their good-byes last night, I realized that Cole and Lara were the first of "mine" that I will never see again in this life. Erica may get to return. The pain is unbearable. Cindy and I dissolved into wet washrags, and still today, the pain is exquisite. There are no tears here, just floods. Good-bye, Cole and Lara. Opa loves you so very much.

(Long pause.)

Cindy and I absolutely love reading your comments in the guestbook, as it is much more personal than any e-mail. Please keep them coming if you can. I see each of your faces as I read. It is a blessing that so many here do not have. Thank you, Lord, for the pleasure of really knowing these friends. Thank you for spreading the burden over their shoulders as well as mine. I am blessed with memories no one can erase, memories I will bring back to heaven with me. Thank you, dear friends.

MIDDLESEX HOSPICE

WRITTEN NOVEMBER 21, 2011, 9:25 P.M.

Good evening, all. It has been a good day in hospice at Middlesex Hospital. The people here try their best to make your day as pleasant as possible by using both their skilled intellect and their compassionate minds. There are many skills exhibited, and yet their human shortcomings still show through to make us comfortable that they are sharing some of themselves in this end game. They care.

Today, from a medical standpoint, they are chasing my insulin needs. The meds I am on for cancer are designed to help me breath better, reduce inflammation, and keep the pain under control.

Actually, pain control to date has been the easiest issue. I have a pressure that lies right under your hand when you say the pledge of allegiance. When the pressure starts to bother ... more morphine. It's that simple, and to date, I don't use enough of it to make me crazy. The difficult issue is the insulin number. For most healthy people, insulin is measured down around 80 to 125. Mine has been running away with me ... as high as 570. At that number, I bite children. I am not responsible for broken furniture, and I'm really no fun to be around. I remember little of what is said, and by the looks I get from Cindy, it is a good thing that she has a forgiving Christian heart. I apologize for anyone who sees me in that state. For two days, we have been using fast-acting insulin to try to lasso this beast. Now I am using combinations of both fast and Lantus (slow-acting). My insulin level has been waffling back and forth between 500 and about 350. The doctors are willing to allow a base number in the 200s.

Cindy and I also met with one of the social workers here. They are here to share their insights on what is happening, and I think they are a very valuable asset to be used to keep your head screwed on tight. I mentioned it somewhere—maybe in this blog—that this hospice departure is so different from normal earthly death. If your mom or dad, relative or friend dies, people cry, plans are rushed together, obits written, and wham, one more bites the dust. Everyone is in a state of shock, but it's done. In hospice, no one else is sick. The hospice patient must deal with his or her entire inventory of friends dying at once! When a loved one leaves my room, I expect not to see them again. My grandkids leaving last night and returning to Minneapolis really meant that I would never see them again here on earth. When that happened, I was shocked, and even though I have been living with the idea of hospice and thought I knew what was happening. I am through that now, but holy moly, both Cindy and I were caught by surprise.

Back on the "blog," I think we all are seeing changes in people as they have the opportunity to process information that they may have never heard of before.

I am excited because the Middlesex Hospice Unit is providing me with a room for our men's Bible study and a pizza snack on Wednesday night, and they are going to check me out and in for Thanksgiving dinner. They have raised their power setting to "maximum warp" in order to support their patient. me.

I feel special. Thank you, Middlesex.

TESTIFY, LEE STROBEL!

WRITTEN NOVEMBER 22, 2011, 9:46 P.M.

I'm thrilled that for the last two hours I have been on the stand, witnessing to one of the technicians here. I am asking her to read *A Case for Christ*. She has had no contact with any "religion" since her parents became disenchanted twenty-five years ago. She is interested and definitely seeking. Fun stuff!

WRITTEN NOVEMBER 23, 2011, 5:31 P.M.

Another great day at hospice. Looks like I will be getting out of here tomorrow morning, even though we are still fighting to get control of the insulin numbers. Since Sunday morning, we have been chasing numbers that vary between 280 and 500. Each day, we seem to see or at least want to see some progress, and each day, we seem to be snookered by one chemical or another. The good news is that it really doesn't matter. The end result will be the same. The date is the only thing that can change, and I really don't care much about the end date. We have already celebrated a small Christmas with my grandchildren and bought Charlie Brown trees for my "man-cave." Heck, I even have a small tree that plugs into my USB port on my laptop, and I have fiber optics changing colors in the branches. It's fun.

As I mentioned, tomorrow, I get out. Tonight, I am looking forward to hosting with Rich Pancoast our regular Wednesday-night men's Bible study—except tonight is happening in Middlesex Hospital in the hospice ward. I am thrilled to be able to do this with the men. We are taking over in a nice way the family room for an hour or so. We will need to understand that the primary purpose of that room is to serve the families who are going through one of the most important times of their lives as they assist their loved ones to give up the life they knew and to transition to an eternal existence somewhere. Ours is a glad coming to this place. There are many families that are in the deepest, darkest depths they have ever known. I think that episode Cindy and I had when we sent our grandchildren back to Minneapolis was a God-sent reminder to us of the pain that can exist in a place like this.

My own experience here has been beautiful. I could not have asked for a more wonderful place to come for treatment. My only sadness is that I have not found this place as a place to volunteer with. There are many people who contribute time and effort to assist in supplying basic companionship, conversation, and comfort. These are the unsung heroes of hospice, the folks who come without being asked. I sit in awe of their dedication to the job at hand.

So tonight, a dozen or so men come to support me. I have asked their help in "finishing well." I can't wait to tell them the real story. More later.

AND THE EPILOGUE ... 11:00 P.M., WEDNESDAY

WRITTEN NOVEMBER 23, 2011, 10:57 P.M.

Remember snuggling into your mom's arms after a busy day? Enough popcorn and ice cream?

Our men's group rocked tonight from the seventh floor of the Middlesex Hospital. Men from all over Middlesex County came together in a common interest, willing to declare themselves all connected by one God, who is our best friend. I love you guys. Thank you for your support. The tape recording worked well. I will just need to address levels a little, and then I will get a copy to Rich, who will distribute it. I am fatigued but very, very satisfied with our time together. I am looking forward to eternity spent like that, with God as our teacher, slowly peeling back the layers of fog that have covered our eyes. The mysteries of the ages will be mine soon. Are you jealous?

THANKSGIVING DAY

WRITTEN NOVEMBER 24, 2011, 6:13 P.M.

We enjoyed a wonderful Thanksgiving dinner at Rich and Vic's house today, even though the hospital is still chasing my insulin needs down. I am finding out way too much about this stuff and feel sorrier for diabetics every moment. The disease can knock you down in a second and unfortunately can alter your state of mind remarkably. The good doctors would be satisfied with me in the 200s somewhere, maybe even the low 300s, but this 400 and 500 stuff is in need of careful watching. And I hope *not* in the hospital. My room was great, but as Dorothy said, "There's no place like home."

Cindy had my man-cave room all set up with flowers. (stinky, so out they went!) and other comforts like double urinals, man-sized walkers, twenty-gallon garbage can for empty pop cans and TV/

VCR controls at arm's reach. She has peeled some grapes for me and is waving a ostrich feather over my head to keep the one fruit fly way that came in with the grapes.

Yeah, life is good in Durham ... just a little south of the *Twilight Zone*.

FUN YESTERDAY

WRITTEN NOVEMBER 26, 2011, 6:28 A.M.

So yesterday was a fun day. My daughter, Erica, drove all the way from Minneapolis to Durham in a VW Jetta, with her dog and a great guy who did most of the driving for her. (Thanks, Dave.) Dave will be flying back to Minneapolis but return again for Erica afterward to get her home. Adam is flying out here from Oregon in a week or so. Beth is flying in from Austin, TX, when it is her turn to babysit.

I am weaker than I thought I would become this soon. Erica's nurse friend seems to have been right. God has got me all sewed up on the spiritual side, and I am so content there. The medical side is another thing—weakness, weakness, weakness. I am having a hard time lifting my legs to get pajamas on, and a good shower, while still very refreshing, is a grueling job. Thank you, Cindy! I never thought that I would have to start thinking about home health aides to help me bathe. Hey, guys, stick with me here. I am giving you all the news, good or bad, and I need your help here to finish well. I cherish your guestbook entries beyond understanding, and I read them many times daily, thinking of your faces and feeling warm that you care enough to write. There is no little word that you say that I don't appreciate greatly. Please keep it coming.

Hey, I have some good news to share. Durham has been our home since 1981. Pretty soon, I understand, that time frame will qualify us as locals, not quite a long-term residents. Well, Durham is aware of the good things that have happened in town during those years, and Durham offers a very special program for retired seniors on inflexible incomes. Cindy and I fall into that category. We live on social security and a few pensions picked up along the way, along with life's dwindling savings. In Durham, if your income qualifies and one homeowner is over sixty-five, application may be made to "freeze" property taxes at the current level. We are working with the town now on the details but want to shout out the good service we are getting, and we look forward to being enrolled shortly. Thank you, Durham. Thank you, Laura Francis, for darn good social policy. I am proud to be a resident of Durham.

Almost 7:00 a.m., blood test time. By the way, those tiny spikes that you send into your finger three or four times per day do start to hurt after a couple of weeks. No real biggie here, but still a pain.

Looking forward to a couple of nice visits today: Cindy's first online supermarket shopping, Nephew Kurt, and family, and a meal along the way from one of our favorite comfort food technicians.

Prayer for today

Father, Abba, I am who am, bless these times. Open our eyes to the reality of the moments we live in. Examine your people and give each the skills, the work ethic, the charity, and the love to serve others. Let local churches remove the blinders of selfishness and see the local need. May they step boldly into a system of giving that emboldens their members to do more because it is right and because of the blessings you bestow. Amen.

WRITTEN NOVEMBER 28, 2011, 11:38 A.M.

So many things to consider. This hospice program encourages self-involvement and decision-making. Obviously, they offer a whole palate of drugs and directions on their use, but still, there is a greater freedom as you search for that combination that will best serve your particular lifestyle.

I felt absolutely terrible on last Saturday night when I was admitted. I had taken some drugs that brought me back in line. I could breath again. I could carry on a conversation again, but I also gave up some of my self. I could understand some of what my own grandchildren were saying to me, and my answers to them were drugged. My stay in the hospital was used to chase the crazy sugar numbers around, and I cannot tell you how frustrating that was. I, Capt. Bob, used to being in control. What the heck was going on?

Vicki's Thanksgiving dinner helped a lot. I needed to get grounded in family, and it was a wonderful day, Vic! The struggle went on though. High sugar? Lower it. Do it again. Prick your fingers until you can't find a spot to do it.

I finally was able to get out of there on Thanksgiving, and I promptly took myself "off" of all "as needed" pills. Those included the morphine and a sedative that bothered me.

I finally scheduled a family meeting as I couldn't be trusted to make these drug decisions. I was experiencing panic attacks and needed some concrete decisions made. Vicki, Rich, Erica, Cindy, and Dave met with me, and after we set up the ground rules, we battled it out. (I would agree to consensus, and they would take every word I said seriously.) The stumbling block seemed to be a drug called lorazapam. It is an antianxiety drug that, when partnered up with morphine, is supposed to do wonders for my breathing. Well, even at the one-milligram level, it knocked me right out. For those of you who saw me in church on Sunday, you saw the worst. I wasn't awake half the time, didn't recognize people, and generally got very little from a visit that was very hard to pull off. It was only later in the day when the drug wore off that I had a wonderful afternoon with my family. The family met again, and we are now splitting the pills into fourths. Cindy and/or Erica are giving me small quantities during the night at 3:30 a.m., and I am eating breakfast precisely at 6:00 a.m., all in order to ward off these panic attacks. It seems to be working. At least it is so far today.

Prayer

Lord God, bless families who care for their loved ones. Give wives super strength in times of need. May they take comfort in the knowledge that they do God's work when they comfort the sick. May they find other family and dedicated friends to care for them in their time. May they forge strong bonds with you as days count down, and my special prayer for all reading this blog is that they look you squarely in the eye and commit themselves fully to your invitation of undying love. Amen.

PS: Cole and Lara, Bennett and Sadie, Opa loves you so much!

MORE HISTORY

WRITTEN NOVEMBER 29, 2011, 6:38 A.M.

Another day that hopes to go well. I woke up this morning with a 253 number. Usually, that indicates a good day coming. Thank you, Jesus, for another day to visit with friends, smile, and cry with them.

I have turned into a real wet washcloth. Sort of the way the wizard of Oz cried in the movie. On, off, on, off. My social worker from hospice did a good job explaining it, but I have forgotten what she said. Once she said even strong men had to have emotional releases, I was good to go.

I am looking forward to seeing one of my favorite people in town. Karen serves as the Democrat registrar of voters, and I served as Republican registrar. Very unlikely "bedfellows," but a team that worked not only for the town but for Middlesex County. For three years or so (until my sickness), we cochaired the county organization as well, and attendance kept increasing until now. We can expect upward of twenty registrars in attendance at the meetings. There is a place for politics, but not inside the registrar's office at town hall. It's is a laugh when we go to a convention, and both Karen and I are given the floor in turn. We are absolute opposites arguing a question, and when done, we sit back down and have lunch together at our table. Good stuff, and both sides get heard in an open-aired setting.

Karen's son, Matthew, has an idea or two to get onto video tape for school. We also would like to ask for folks to consider volunteering to act as poll workers. Our current dedicated force numbers about eighteen with an average age in the mid- to late-seventies, and they work an eighteen-hour day, all the while claiming to love the job! Help!

WRITTEN NOVEMBER 30, 2011, 3:52 P.M.

Okay. First, make believe that I had written a really upbeat journal entry today, and then when I got a surprise phone call, I lost the whole thing. You would have loved it. *Well, that is exactly what happened! Thanks, Mike!*

The messages I get via CaringBridge still sustain us here. You are visiting the sick, hugging me, and surrounding me with your love. I am praying for each of you that the clarity I enjoy with my relationship with God will present itself to you in your sure-to-come time of need. I call you all friends, and should we not get together before my end, please understand that Cindy and I spend wonderful times together in prayer for you and for your families. What happened to me here needs to be shared and multiplied, and that is the best part. It is boundlessly available for the asking and the praying to our Lord and Savior, Jesus Christ.

Good things did happen today, and I am more upbeat than I have been in days. My heart problems (atrial fibrillation) really exacerbated my cancer symptoms, and I was blaming a lot of my sudden weakness to cancer instead on the fact that I have about half the lung power I used to have to drive this manly body around. The nurse was funny as she took my pulse. She finally recorded it as a range of a hundred to 153 in random beats. It was laughable. I sounded more like an African drum ensemble than a human.

So looks like we can make it to December. Wouldn't it be great to make Christmas after all?

FRIENDS, LOVERS, AND GOD

WRITTEN DECEMBER 1, 2011, 3:50 A.M.

My days are filled with friends, lovers, and God.

Friends

The outpouring from my friends of sentiment, well-wishes, and people "wantin' summa what I got" is amazing. I testify to you that we people are wonderfully built by God and have incredible communication ability when we take the time to rise to the level of human participation, where the veils come down, the smoke and mirrors disappear, a tear might flow and where we open ourselves to the pain of introspection, which allows an openness of mind to accepting new thoughts of love and vulnerability. We all begin to get the look of "the deer in the headlights." We become open for something beyond the norm. We become open for serious conversation. I love serious conversation, and I confess that I wish I knew that before now. Maybe you, who are blessed with longer agendas, can work on those conversations to have with your own friends.

Lovers

Lovers are special. For me, they include my wife, my children, my brothers Frank and Joe, and my baby sister, Ann. My nephews, nieces, and their children all seem to have grasped onto this situation. Also, I must include my special friend from childhood Paulie. K. and my spiritual mentor Pastor S. I know I have other lovers as well. My Bible study men's group prayed and cried with me. They may never know how powerful that meeting was at hospice. Sorry, guys, but you might be one of my lovers. Back to that hospice meeting. It was huge to me and a major comfort as I approach the stadium for the two-lap finish. My personal Olympics marathon nears the end, and the with God's help, the victory is assured.

God, Jesus Christ, Holy Spirit

He was born in an obscure village, the child of a peasant woman. He grew up in still another village, where He worked in a carpenter shop until He was thirty. Then for three years, He was an itinerant preacher. He never wrote a book. He never held an office. He never had a family or owned a house. He didn't go to college. He never traveled more than two hundred miles from the place He was born. He did none of the things one usually associates with greatness. He had no credentials but Himself. He was only thirty-three when public opinion turned against Him. His friends deserted Him. He was turned over to His enemies and went through the mockery of a trial. He was nailed to a cross between two thieves. When He was dying, His executioners gambled for His clothing, the only property He had. ... on earth. When He was dead, He was laid in a borrowed grave through the pity of a friend. Nineteen centuries have come and gone, and today, He is the central figure of the human race, the leader of mankind's progress. All the armies that ever marched, all the navies that ever sailed, all the parliaments that ever sat, all the kings that ever reigned, all these put together have not affected the life of man on earth as much as that one solitary life. *Do you know who He is?*

Taken from "One Solitary Life Poem" by Dr. James Allan 1926

I have had the privilege of actually sealing a contract with my creator. Maybe I can explain.

My "religious" and educational history included thirteen years of religious school and about thirty years of wandering around and listening to talk radio on religion while I "worked" my way through divorce and disappointment in organized "religion." I thought I was a good guy, and I thought when the big creator in the sky pushed the subtotal button, I would qualify for salvation and a heavenly home address. I was trying to "work my way to heaven" and maybe even trying to sneak in by being just good enough. I would have strong feelings toward God followed by the times the Devil tempting me with doubt. Sinful thoughts, words, and deeds winged like vultures over my head at times. I was human. I was confused. I so wanted to be sure of my salvation. I so wanted to have some sort of a sign.

It was at that time that I read *A Case for Christ*, a great book by Lee Strobel. I also began a relationship with Fellowship Church and got to know both pastors, father and son, Steve and Andy Eiss. Steve and I were aged appropriately, and we became workout partners at the gym that my son-in-law managed. Spiritually, I was challenged by an event on the boat I was captaining. A passenger OD'ed on board a charter evening cruise. I was presented with whether this man went to heaven or hell. He sure as heck was dead. As a Catholic, I was taught with suicide, you're in hell. As a Christian, more goes into it. It is not for us to know the will of God. It is not for us to be judgmental. It is not for us to draw up our own picture of God's actions. We cannot invent any part of God. That would be creating an idol and thus becoming an idol worshiper.

My contract with God began when I realized that I had to be responsible for my own relationship with a personal God, Jesus Christ, the God that did all the work on the cross freely. He did it as a gift for me, no strings attached. That was his side of the contract. My side was that I had to accept His love as a gift and acknowledge that I had no part in the miracle it created. My deal with Christ was that I had to get to the point where I laid *all* of my chips on the table and said a simple prayer: "Not my will but Thy will be done." That, my dear friends, was a difficult place to get to. I had to trust Jesus Christ in all decisions, and I failed and failed and failed; however, through my church, I found support among my fellow church people. We were all sinners as it turned out, and we were all seeking. We built relationships and strengthened each other. It was not until my cancer developed late in 2009 that the idea of mortality came home. I was given about a 20 to 25 percent chance of five-year survival, which makes a guy really think. Six or seven months ago when the thing came back full force, I really had to deal with this whole mortality thing. Finally, with the second lung operation, the doctors did the answering for my questions. There was no further treatment available to cure this cancer. One after the other, the doctors conveyed their chagrin to me, but I was a goner.

Meanwhile, back with God, His contract still was offering me heaven through surrender. God gave me an opportunity to throw in all the chips and ride shotgun with Him. The rest is for history. It would take a book to get it all down, a book that I don't have time for now but a book that maybe someone can piece together out of the ramblings of my blog.

I can only tell you this: I am so grateful to God that He gave me this cancer. In a few days, weeks, or months, I will be with Him, learning the mysteries of the ages. Hopefully, I'll be hugging my mom in my arms, being able to pray for my family on earth, and enjoying what I see. Life is so temporary. We all are terminal. I just had a shorter time of it than you do.

I am tired now, so I will say good day. I will be on the job tonight, praying for all of you. I pray that you are able to provide for your families spiritually and financially, that God blesses you with love, children, and especially grace. I pray that you will be able to have enough faith in God to make that first big step across that bridge separating you from Him. Remember that our gift to God is faith, and His immediate gift back is grace. Go for it. It's well worth it.

GOOD!

WRITTEN DECEMBER 2, 2011, 4:52 P.M.

I won't beat around the bush today, guys. I had a great day. The meds seemed to line up with my needs, and aside from the slow weakening I feel from time to time, I am very satisfied.

I am at peace with myself, my cancer, and my creator. I could not be having a better day!

WRITTEN DECEMBER 3, 2011, 7:48 A.M.

Sugar low at 209. Great! Feel great! Great breakfast!

How sweet it seems for me to marvel near the end of life that God has time to hold my hand as we journey toward the light. His gift to *us* is eternal life. Just commit to make the change. "Surrender, Bob, surrender all. My promises I keep."

Pray to Him personally. Right now is best. Tell Him that you love Him and ask His forgiveness.

Heavenly Father, have mercy on me, a sinner. I believe in you and that your word is true. I believe that Jesus Christ is the Son of the living God and that He died on the cross so that I may now have forgiveness for my sins and eternal life. I know that without you in my heart my life is meaningless.

I believe in my heart that you, Lord God, raised Him from the dead. Please, Jesus, forgive me for every sin I have ever committed or done in my heart. Please, Lord Jesus, forgive me and come into my heart as my personal Lord and Savior today. I need you to be my Father and my friend.

I give you my life and ask you to take full control from this moment on. I pray this in the name of Jesus Christ.

Amen.

Friends, if you prayed that prayer with me today, you have brought me great pleasure, not pleasure that is fleeting and needs to be renewed by some sort of human "fix" but rather a pleasure that will last forever as we will be in heaven for eternity. *That's one more for Jesus.*

WRITTEN DECEMBER 3, 2011, 8:18 P.M.

Trying to keep it light today, folks.

Bit of a tough day starting at noon on December 3rd. I was tired this morning and had screwed up body functions this afternoon. Experienced great weakness in legs and difficulty moving about the house. Cindy and others followed me around with a seated walker so that if I needed to bail out on my legs, I had a place to land. I couldn't sit in any low chairs, as I couldn't get back up again.

Still planning on church tomorrow. Hope to be there for the ending of the 9:30. Plan to meet up with Ben Eiss. Then after church, I'm looking forward to seeing Bob and Andrew Moore. Cindy and the MAPS crew are serving ice cream for the annual MAPS Christmas Party, but Rich is taking me home and babysitting. I no longer can be left alone.

The transition that I am going through is not hard. Not knowing what to expect is the hard part.

My friends continue to strengthen me with well-wishes and visits. I love the attention. What I don't like is some of the attention that I get relative to my conversations with you about God. He has chosen to use me as a type of tool to demonstrate what He can do. Maybe you can think of me more like a "Vegematic food slicer"—really cool to use but just a chunk of plastic in the hands of a master. God is offering you and me that chance of a lifetime to embrace His plan and spend the rest of eternity with Him in paradise. He just made it easier for me by handing me cancer to deal with. He only is asking me to get a grasp on the obvious and has made it easy for me to surrender to His will.

I am having fun now. I have a virtual prayer cannon, and I use it to surprise the unexpected. A disguised superhuman figure, Captain Bob waits quietly in dark alleys and in unsuspecting localities, just waiting for someone to come along needing a prayer. After he carefully loads the prayer cannon, he fires for effect and more often than not knocks the Devil right off the unsuspecting sinner's shoulder. It's fun helping out where I can, and some of those devils put on a good show falling back to Hades, where they belong. Bob was once heard saying that he hasn't had as much fun since he was shooting rats in the dumps outside Lake Shawnee in New Jersey fifty-five years ago.

Have a great night. Say your prayers and an extra one for someone else. Remember, "One more for Jesus."

WRITTEN DECEMBER 5, 2011, 3:59 A.M.

Going to be taking it easy today, guys. I was really logy yesterday and slept half of it away. By the way, my daughter Erica's pulled pork sandwiches came out fabulous, so let me know if you want to try the mildest, most scrumptious pulled pork.

Leftovers today. Sorry, Scott. Won't last until dinner.

Erica has taken over the meds department, and we have been known to crash in the past, so the first logical suspect would be her, my friends.

WRITTEN DECEMBER 8, 2011, 7:08 A.M.

Things are getting more difficult now. More care coming on board. Cindy can't handle my needs. Thank God for Erica and Vicki as well as my oldest friend, Paulie from California.

Christmas is a real question mark now. I love you all. Please don't call. Please pray. I/we are fine, but this is ours now. If there is anything you can assist us with, we will surely call you.

My joyful prayers!

WRITTEN DECEMBER 12, 2011, 11:42 A.M. BY ERICA SCHULTE

Dear family and friends,

We wanted to update everyone on Dad's condition. Over the last couple days, we have witnessed a great decline in his cognitive abilities. He has few moments of clarity, and he is entering a different stage. After a family meeting and speaking with the hospice nurse, we as a family have decided he would benefit from hospital hospice care. This was a difficult decision, as we hoped we would be able to care for him at home; however, it has become increasingly difficult, and to our surprise, he is declining very rapidly.

The family is not accepting visitors at this time, and please do not call, as he is often unable to communicate effectively and sleeps often. We appreciate all your love and support, and please continue to communicate your posts in the guestbook. We will update you as soon as we can.

Erica, Adam, Vicki, Beth, and Cindy

WRITTEN DECEMBER 16, 2011, 10:31 A.M.

BY VICTORIA PANCOAST

Hi, all,

Bob wanted me to write today and let you know that he is so grateful for your love and prayers. He is weaker but still has moments of clarity, and we are enjoying the time we have with him.

In his words, "I am blissfully aware of the blessings that I receive daily. My life has been absolutely wonderful. I love all of my grandchildren. I am so thankful for my family and especially the wonderful times we have had in the last few weeks. Love one another, and I will see you soon."

WRITTEN DECEMBER 24, 2011, 6:24 A.M.

BY VICTORIA PANCOAST

Captain Bob Schulte entered into the presence of the Lord at 4:00 a.m. on December 24, 2011.

"To be absent from the body is to be present with the Lord" (2 Corinthians 5:8 (NKJV)).

When details are decided for his service, we will post them here and in the local papers. In lieu of flowers, we have set up the "Captain Bob Living Proof Memorial Fund" at Fellowship Church in Middletown, CT. This fund will benefit the teens at church, the kids learning about Christ whom Bob put his heart and soul into supporting.

WE MISS YOU, CAPTAIN BOB.

WRITTEN DECEMBER 27, 2011, 9:20 A.M.

BY VICTORIA PANCOAST

Robert R. Schulte, 65 of Durham, CT, beloved husband of Lucinda (Cindy) Schulte, entered into the presence of his Savior on Saturday December 24th 2011 at Middlesex Hospital.

He was born in Montclair, NJ, as the son of Herman J. and Helen (Hempen) Schulte. He worked in sales for many years at Stanley Tools and later was Director of Sales for Merillat Industries before retiring in 2000. In his retirement, Bob became "Captain Bob" and pursued his love of boating. In recent years, Captain Bob lived his dream as Lead Captain for the Essex Steam Train and Riverboat Company and served as a liaison between the company and the US Coast Guard.

Besides his wife, he is survived by his four children: Adam Schulte of Medford, OR; Erica Schulte of Minneapolis, MN; Beth Puorro of Austin, TX; and Victoria (Puorro) Pancoast of Middletown, CT. In addition, he leaves his brothers, Frank Schulte and Joe Schulte, both of NJ, and his sister, Ann Schulte Steimle of Lumberland, NY. He was an amazing grandfather to his four grandchildren: Cole, Lara, Bennett, and Sadie, and they will always remember him as Opa.

In lieu of flowers, donations can be sent directly to Fellowship Church, 1002 Saybrook Road, Middletown, CT 06457, for the "Captain Bob Living Proof Memorial Fund." This fund will benefit the teens at church, a cause that Captain Bob supported with his heart and soul. Please make checks out to Fellowship Church with "Captain Bob" in the memo line.

The memorial service will be held at Fellowship Church on Saybrook Road in Middletown at 12:00 p.m. on Saturday, January 7, 2012.

Chapter 10

Closing Prayer

Written February 15, 2012, 7:43 p.m. by Cindy Schulte

I sit here tonight, realizing that I need to end this CaringBridge with a prayer of thanks to God and to all the people who have shared in this incredible journey. I am preparing to put this into book form but wanted to end it with overwhelming thanks and praise to all! It has been a tremendous journey, one that will continue ... in my heart forever.

God worked through Bob to show us all how to accept death. Each day, he spoke to Jesus (sitting right next to him) and told us how much he felt God's presence. I am missing him terribly but know that God's timing is always correct. I know that God is with me and will keep me strong and help me find my purpose for the future. I am constantly hearing the stories of how Bob's CaringBridge has helped you. Carry it with you. God bless you all.

Cindy